NOT ANOTHER BROKE ATHLETE

NOT ANOTHER BROKE ATHLETE

A Simple and Straightforward Plan
to Keep and Grow the Money You Earn

DON PADILLA CFP®
AND SHKIRA SINGH

NEW YORK

NASHVILLE • MELBOURNE • VANCOUVER

NOT ANOTHER BROKE ATHLETE

A Simple and Straightforward Plan to Keep and Grow the Money You Earn

Published in New York, New York, by Morgan James Publishing. Morgan James is a trademark of Morgan James, LLC. www.MorganJamesPublishing.com

The Morgan James Speakers Group can bring authors to your live event. For more information or to book an event visit The Morgan James Speakers Group at www.TheMorganJamesSpeakersGroup.com.

ISBN 9781683504740 paperback
ISBN 9781683503910 eBook
Library of Congress Control Number: 2016920960

Cover and Interior Design by:
Chris Treccani
www.3dogcreative.net

In an effort to support local communities, raise awareness and funds, Morgan James Publishing donates a percentage of all book sales for the life of each book to Habitat for Humanity Peninsula and Greater Williamsburg.

Get involved today! Visit
www.MorganJamesBuilds.com

TABLE OF CONTENTS

Introduction   *Just Another Statistic*   *xi*

Chapter 1   Why Do Professional Athletes Go Broke?   1

Chapter 2   The Psychology, Flow, and Soul of Money   27

Chapter 3   Know Your Finances   47

Chapter 4   Seek Counsel, Not Advice   65

Chapter 5   Is There Life After Sports?   75

Chapter 6   The Essentials of Starting a Business   93

Acknowledgments   *113*

About Don Padilla   *119*

About Shkira Singh   *121*

As an athlete, you only have so much time. The window only has so much time and then it closes. You have to take care of yourself the best you can.

—BARRY BONDS

Just Another Statistic

—

A TALE OF TWO ATHLETES

Billy had been "the star" since he could walk. He was the kind of natural athlete who seemed destined to be in the limelight. From the moment he first picked up a football, he knew he'd found his calling—and so did his parents and everyone who saw him play. He loved every minute of it. Sure, there was school, family and friends, but at the end of the day, all that mattered was the game. He dedicated his body and his mind to the sport and became so hardwired for training, practicing, and game time situations, that everything else was just, well, background noise.

Billy spent the prime years of his life training to become a world-class athlete, and all his hard work eventually paid off in a big way. He was chosen in the first round of the draft by the team he'd always dreamed of playing for. This was it. Every drop of blood, sweat, and tears over the last twenty-one years…it all culminated into that moment.

He had made it. He was somebody…somebody who was about to get paid millions of dollars to play a game he loved and cherished.

The first few years were like a dream. His name was on the back of kids' jerseys across the country. Endorsement deals were flying at him faster than he could accept them. His life was all about catching footballs, listening to the cheering crowds, meeting fans, partying at the most exclusive locations, and buying fast cars and big houses. *He truly was living the dream.*

But then his fourth season came along—and so did a career-ending injury. And just like that, it was all over. No more running out of the tunnel onto the field to the sound of the deafening crowds. No one was asking for his autograph. In an instant, no one cared about him anymore.

At the age of twenty-five, Billy found himself without a career, without a future, and ultimately, without an identity. Thanks to his careless spending habits and lack of knowledge about his finances, he was also dead broke within a short time after his untimely exit from the game, and he was now working at a grocery store.

It had never occurred to him, that he'd be faced with sixty-plus years left to live once his career was over. As he left the stadium locker room for the final time with the remnants of a lost career in his hands, he thought miserably to himself:

WHAT AM I GOING TO DO?

Keith was a quiet child. Growing up poor, he always imagined what his life would have been like on the other side of the tracks. Keith wasn't the kind of guy to sit around and dream. Like Billy, he also had determination and drive. He may not have been a true "natural," but he was willing to put in the work to succeed at any cost.

He saved up enough money from doing odd jobs around the neighborhood to buy his very first bat and glove. From that point on, he put everything he had into making it one day. He studied hard in school, and he practiced every bit as hard. Keith knew that nothing in life is given, and he wanted to ensure that his children would never know the want that he had grown accustomed to as a child. This is why he decided he would be the very best student he could be just in case he didn't get a baseball scholarship.

He got that scholarship—and was off to Arizona State University, a famous baseball school thanks to his good grades and high test scores. Four years later, he was drafted and shortly after, he was playing in the majors. His name was never on any billboards. He didn't get any big endorsement deals. In fact, given the country's mistaken idea that every player gets paid untold millions of dollars, most people would be shocked to find out that his salary was in the much lower end of seven figures. It was certainly more money than most people make, but according to professional sports standards, Keith's salary was on the low end of average.

Keith felt rich beyond his wildest dreams, and he immediately began setting up his finances and his estate. He set up his financial future in a way that it continued to make money for him long after he'd smack his final fastball. He purchased a home in a modest upper middle class neighborhood, drove a new Toyota, and sent his children to private school. Most of his neighbors didn't even know he was a pro baseball player. Keith and his wife planned one vacation a year, while he stashed money away for retirement and his kids' college funds.

Four years into his career, he was traded to a new team, and three seasons later, due to some chronic knee pain, he decided to retire. He'd had a respectable career, but it was time to put his business degree to good use. As he hung up his jersey for the final time, he thought expectantly to himself:

WHAT WILL I DO NEXT?

No one ever thinks he or she will end up like Billy, and yet his fate is not an uncommon one for professional athletes across all sports. The reason is simple: Financial problems do not discriminate—they do not care whether you are male or female, grew up poor or rich, or play football, tennis, hockey, volleyball, or basketball. If you don't plan for *life after sports*, you will be facing a very grim reality not long after your retirement.

A 2009 *Sports Illustrated* study, revealed that after only two years of retirement, 78 percent of NFL players were either broke or struggling financially, and within five years of retirement, 60 percent of NBA players are broke.[1] Those are some staggering numbers for athletes. It means that their almost predictable future is that they will be among those players who look back on their short-lived career and end up like Billy, wondering, "What am I going to do?"

It's tempting to look at a big salary and think, "I'll be set for life with that kind of money coming in!" But *NOBODY* is set for life without proper financial planning and execution. The good news is that you don't have to be a statistic or just another cautionary tale—and that's why we are here today. You CAN make the kinds of choices that Keith made with self-awareness and proper guidance.

And it's easier than you think.

---

1   Torre, Pablo S. "How (and Why) Athletes Go Broke." *Sports Illustrated*, March 23, 2009. Print.

THE ROAD TO MY "WHY"

Years ago, I almost became my own kind of statistic. There I was, living in Oxnard, California, struggling to eke out an existence with my mother and her *new* husband. My mother was about to make a decision that would change my life, again. It was a decision that she had made before—and I knew the pain of her choice all too well—but this time, for some reason, it felt different.

Her new husband and I didn't get along, and he had given her an ultimatum: "IT'S ME OR YOUR SON." She had made her choice, and sadly, the decision wasn't in my favor.

I couldn't believe she was about to choose "some guy" over her child, just as she had done before. All I had wanted to hear from her was, "No, Donald, you are staying. *He* can leave. You are my son, and I love you!"

But that's _not_ what she said. She was willing to just…let me go. I knew that my mother's choice meant that I'd once again be sleeping on a rolled-up mattress (called a colchon in Spanish) in the living room of my grandmother's home. It wasn't the life I wanted. *None of this is what I wanted.* I snapped out of my thoughts and decided to take matters into my own hands.

I ran up to my stepfather's bedroom door. *BANG, BANG, BANG!* I screamed through the door as I pounded again and again. "GET OUT HERE AND BE A MAN!"

He wasn't about to show his face; he could tell from my voice I wasn't messing around. As I continued banging on the door, my mother yelled at me, "GET OUT AND DON'T COME BACK!"

If she wanted me gone, I wasn't going to go quietly. I ran to my room and threw a 45-pound plate through my window—and then I threw another as glass shattered around me. I grabbed my signed baseball bat (one of my most prized possessions), ran outside, and proceeded to smash the windshield of my stepfather's pickup truck.

At that moment, my best friend Jacob, came racing to my house in his brand new Acura Legend that he bought from his signing bonus from the San Francisco Giants. He took the bat from my hands (the ironic thing was it was a San Francisco Giants Bat signed by him), and calmed me down as only Jacob could. It was only then that I had even realized what had happened. The adrenaline had been rushing through my body, blinding me from all logic and reason.

The anger, rage, hate, and hurt I felt had almost pushed me past the point of no return. If Jacob hadn't taken that bat and pulled me off the ledge, I believe today, I'd be just another statistic, rotting away in prison. But, thanks to the grace of God, today I am a successful business owner, speaker, author, mentor, and most importantly, a husband and father to two beautiful children.

Without Jacob's interference, I know my story would have had a very different ending. Since then, I have been able to heal and renew the relationship with my mom. All is forgiven, and I'm still here and not in a prison cell. I've been privileged to be able to make a difference in the lives of many people from every background and every walk of life. That is how I found my *why*—my experiences made me realize that my true calling is to be an educator, speaker, mentor and advisor to those who have at the highest risk of self-sabotage in their lives due to a reason to which I can truly relate: They weren't taught a better way by others in their younger years.

And that is why I help professional athletes
—and really, anyone looking for financial answers—
to find that better way.

My counsel is not filled with economic jargon or complex formulas. It is simple and straightforward information that you will learn from this book. This book which is meant to open your eyes, educate you, and ultimately give you confidence to master your financial future.

There is no rulebook that says you have to spend all your money when you get it. There is also no rulebook that says you will be broke within a few years of retiring from sports. In another words . . .

You *don't* have to be a statistic.

And you *don't* have to be "ANOTHER BROKE ATHLETE!"

You're a person a lot longer before and after you're a professional athlete. People always say to me, "Your image is this, your image is that." Your image isn't your character. Character is what you are as a person. That's what I worry about.

—DEREK JETER

1

Why Do Professional Athletes Go Broke?

—

When you think of the most famous athletes from back in the day, what names come to mind? For most of us, names like Babe Ruth, Roberto Clemente, Muhammad Ali, Wilt Chamberlain, and Jesse Owens are obvious choices—and each of these greats will live forever in the annals of sports history and legend.

I have another question for you. *Do you know how much money these legendary athletes made?* Adjusted for inflation, Babe Ruth's highest salary was just $1.4 million—and he was the highest paid player in professional baseball for decades.[2]

---

2   Calcaterra, Craig. "Adjusted for inflation, Babe Ruth's highest salary was $1.4 million." *NBC Sports Hardball Talk*. NBC, April 2, 2013. Web.

That seems like peanuts now, doesn't it?

Muhammad Ali made considerably more than Babe did, thanks in large part to promoters like the infamous Don King. Muhammad Ali made a total of $40 million in his career. He earned $3 million per fight, and over $5 million in his fight with George Foreman.

Still…only $3 million for a fight? Nowadays, a single heavyweight championship match brings in closer to $30 million or more—and this is often money that is guaranteed—win or lose! In 2012, Oscar de la Hoya received $53 million for his matchup against Floyd Mayweather, Jr.[3] In 2015 Mayweather's fight against Manny Pacquiao earned the boxers a combined pot of $300 million, making Mayweather's career earnings close to a reported $600 million (so far).[4]

The average professional star athlete in the U.S. will make more money in one season than most Americans will make in their entire lives—and that's just an average pro athlete. Top stars like Tiger Woods, LeBron James, and Roger Federer net $50 million or more per year, according to *Forbes*.[5] Despite those amazing salaries, 78 percent of NFL players, 60 percent of NBA players, and a large percentage of MLB players file bankruptcy within five years of retirement.[6]

How can this be??

Over the years, through market research and interviews with athletes, I have identified five major reasons for this epidemic that is running rampant in the world of professional sports. If these issues are not addressed, it doesn't matter how much money athletes make

3   "The Top 10 Highest Paid Boxers of All Time." *The Richest.com*, January 7, 2013. Web.
4   Riccobono, Anthony. "Floyd Mayweather vs. Manny Pacquiao 2015: How Much Money Did the Boxers Make On Saturday?" *International Business Times*, August, 25, 2015. Web.
5   Rankings. "The World's Highest-Paid Athletes." *Forbes*. Forbes, 2015.
6   Preston, Chris. "Five Reasons Professional Athletes Go Broke." *Wyatt Investment Research*. March 25, 2013. Web.

during their careers—they will spend it all and then some, often leaving them worse off than they were before they started playing. Exactly like the "lotto syndrome." Here are the five major reasons why so many of today's professional athletes go broke:

1. Opposite Income Path
2. Living Beyond Their Means (Overspending)
3. Poor Investment Choices
4. Family Pressures
5. Bringing the Wrong People into Their Trusted Circle

As we dig into the reasons, you'll find that each of these underlying causes apply to many different people in a variety of industries and careers. In fact, if you have ever made a lot of money at one time (as in a large bonus), or you made a large sum of money early in life, then this book's message applies directly to you as well.

1. OPPOSITE INCOME PATH

The first hurdle you must overcome, is the fact that your income stream does not flow like the majority. For most of us, we start our careers making the lowest salaries we will ever make, and eventually, with time, effort and experience, we make more and more as we get older. Most Americans' peak earning years are between 40 and 55. According to a recent study conducted by *PayScale*, average men and women see a salary growth of about 60 percent by age thirty.[7]

Professional athletes undergo the exact opposite situation—and for that reason, it is called the Opposite Income Path. They start off their young adult lives—sometimes as young as eighteen years old (and in

---

7   PayScale. "Do Men Really Earn More Than Women? [Infographic]." PayScale. com. Web.

Kobe Bryant's case, seventeen)—making more money than most people will ever see in a lifetime. However, just a few short and explosive years later, they often find themselves without a career and without an income at all. The two diagrams below illustrate the traditional income path versus the opposite income path:

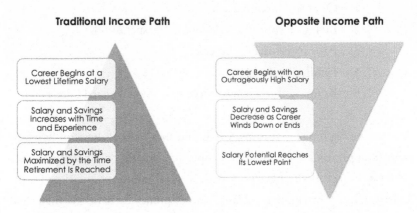

Traditional Income Path

- Career Begins at a Lowest Lifetime Salary
- Salary and Savings Increases with Time and Experience
- Salary and Savings Maximized by the Time Retirement Is Reached

Opposite Income Path

- Career Begins with an Outrageously High Salary
- Salary and Savings Decrease as Career Winds Down or Ends
- Salary Potential Reaches Its Lowest Point

As you can see, athletes experience a salary path that is quite the opposite of the rest of the world. Now, if they are one of the lucky ones, their generous income stream will last maybe seven to ten years. However, with the prevalence of injuries and fickle coaches and owners, most NFL careers last an average of just 3.5 years, NBA careers last 4.8 years on average, and MLB careers are an average of 5.6 years long.[8]

If the rest of the world were only able to hold on to their jobs for five years, they'd be in a whole lot of trouble. But for athletes, they've already made all that money in just a few years, so now they're set for life, right? On the surface, you'd think so. But in reality, they are not. In a traditional income path—where people start working and then continue to consistently work toward retirement 40+ years in the future—you are

---

8   Sandler, Seth. "NFL, MLB, NHL, MLS & NBA: Which Leagues and Players Make the Most Money?" *Bleacher Report*, March 18, 2012. Web.

able to make mistakes and recover. As you get older you begin to save and live more frugally.

This is not the case with most athletes. Hand a wad of cash to a teenager or someone in their twenties and see how long it lasts. Think of the crazy things you did with your money in your 20's, and some people even in their 30's. I even know some people in their 60's still making the same mistakes as they did in their 20's. Well, many professional athletes are just old enough to vote and drink alcohol, and yet they get multimillion dollar contracts. What else would we expect? In short, the Opposite Income Path sets many athletes up for financial failure from the start.

2. LIVING BEYOND YOUR MEANS (OVERSPENDING)

I'm ridin' 'round, I'm gettin' it. I'm ridin' 'round, I'm getting' it. I'm ridin' 'round, I'm gettin' it. It's mine, I spend it. It's mine, I spend it. It's mine, I spend it. It's mine, I spend it…

Those are lyrics from a song called "Spend It" by rapper 2 Chainz. Although the words may seem a bit un-relatable to some, these lyrics echo the truth behind a modern American phenomenon—and that is overspending. Overspending is not just a problem that professional athletes face; it truly is an American problem.

NeighborWorks America, a national nonprofit that supports communities, published a recent survey reporting that the majority of American households (over two-thirds of them) have no *rainy day fund*, otherwise known as a "just in case the sh*t hits the fan fund."[9] Such emergency cash is more formerly known as *liquid reserves*.

Another study from Bankrate.com reported that most of America isn't saving nearly enough. "The best savers are not the highest income households; they're middle income households. Saving is not a function of income. It's a function of having the ability to live within your means and save consistently," says, Greg McBride, Chief Financial Analyst at Bankrate.com.[10]

On a deeper and subconscious level, it comes from "monkey see, monkey do." Even though parents rarely discuss finances with their kids, unless you are aware, you actually become a reflection of your parents. If your parents saved, or handled their finances well, most likely you picked up those tools. If they lived check to check and only paid credit card minimums, chances are you live check to check, doing the same as your parents did. If your parents are still in debt, most likely you will also carry debt. If you are carrying balances on credit cards and short term debt, also known as bad debt, then you are a slave to the dollar.

Jay-Z said it in this verse with DJ Khaled's song, "I Got the Keys!"

*N*ggas always asking me the key*
'Til you own your own you can't be free
'Til you're on your own you can't be me
How we still slaves in 2016?

Although Jay-Z was referring to incarcerations, these verses could also be interpreted being a slave to the almighty dollar. This part of the verse reminds me of the previous NFL football draft. Young men,

---

9   Jones, Charisse. "Millions of Americans have little to no money saved." *USA Today*. USA Today, March 31, 2015. Web.

10   Herron, Janna. "Americans still lack savings despite bigger paychecks." Bankrate. Bankrate.com, March 2015.

that were about to be drafted, and who hadn't signed yet and hadn't even received their first check were already in debt. Some of the future draftees were wearing jewelry worth $100s of thousands of dollars and very expensive suits. Some of these young men were wearing gaudy shoes with spikes with material made from velour—something out of a Liberace costume. They were already in debt trying to outshine each other. I'm not saying you don't want to look good on your big day, but you still want to be conscious of not overspending before you get it. Then what happens is that you feel the pressure to sign the contract just to pay the bills. Proverbs 22:7 in the King James Bible says it best, "The rich ruleth over the poor, and the borrower is servant to the lender."

While this is a common problem in America, it does seem to hit professional athletes even harder. In 2009, *Sports Illustrated* estimated that 78 percent of NFL Players are bankrupt or in some serious financial trouble within two years of retiring. They also estimated that 60 percent of NBA players are broke within five years of retiring from the NBA.[11] Allen Iverson was one of the most influential NBA players of his generation and made over $154 million during his career. Yet, was considered "broke" just a few years out of the league. He was reported to have continued spending over $360,000 a month after his career ended.[12]

Of course, Allen Iverson isn't the first professional athlete to report financial troubles. Many of today's professional athletes come from impoverished or troubled beginnings, and once the money starts rolling in (or even before the money starts rolling in), the lure of spending on luxuries that weren't even imaginable when they were kids is just too strong. Fortunately for Iverson, his former sponsor *Reebok* set up a trust

---

11 Torre, Pablo. "How (and Why) Athletes Go Broke." *Sports Illustrated*. March 23, 2009. Web.

12 Brown, Ann. "Broke Baller: How NBA Star Allen Iverson Lost It All." MadameNoire, May 26, 2015. Web.

fund of $30 million that he won't be able to access until 2030 (when he will be 55 years old).

If only other athletes were so lucky. Mike Tyson, one of the most feared and publicized boxers of all time, made in excess of $400 million during his career. Sadly, just as fast as the money came rolling in, it slipped away. At one point, he had over 200 people employed at his estate, including personal assistants, bodyguards, chauffeurs, chefs, and gardeners. According to bankruptcy court records, in 2003 he paid almost $4.5 million on cars and motorcycles, $3.4 million on clothes and jewelry, $7.8 million on personal expenses, $140,000 on two white Bengal tigers, and $144,000 a year to maintain and care for the tigers. He also bought a $2 million bathtub for first wife, Robin Givens, spent $410,000 on a birthday party, and another $230,000 on cellphones and pagers during a three-year period from 1995 to 1997. "I have been in financial distress since 1998," Tyson said in an affidavit. And according to court documents filed in the divorce case with Givens, he spent $400,000 a month just to maintain his lifestyle.

We've talked a lot about how athletes can spend their millions foolishly, and the common perception is that all athletes are overpaid millionaires—but that's not exactly true. Although there are some superstars like Tiger Woods, LeBron James, and Aaron Rogers that make prolific amounts of money, the vast majority of athletes make far less—and after a short career of being traded around, most of them are not even around long enough to build a large bankroll. Here is a look at the average salaries in professional sports:[13]

---

13   Schwartz, Nick. "The average career earnings of athletes across America's favorite sports will shock you." ForTheWin.com. *USA Today Sports*, Oct 24, 2013. Web.

Professional League		Average Salary
NBA		$5.15 million
MLB		$3.2 million
NHL		$2.4 million
NFL		$1.9 million
Tennis		$0.3 million
MLS		$0.16 million
WNBA		$.075 million

Granted, most of us wouldn't complain about earning $1.9 million or even $750,000 a year, and we'd certainly feel (or should feel) blessed to make that kind of income. The real problem is the "culture of overspending" that runs rampant in our society. Whether athletes make $300,000 or $300 million, there is a pressure that exists in the world of professional sports to flaunt their money with the best cars, jewelry, fashion, and houses that money (or credit) can buy as I previously mentioned before about the draftees. In the end, some of the "average" earners in sports end up with hundreds of thousands of dollars in debt thanks to their need to make it look like they are "ballin out of control."

I had the privilege to ask retired boxer and winner of ten world titles in six different weight classes of Golden Boy Promotions, Oscar De La Hoya, a few questions on the topic of athletes and money:

DON: *Oscar, knowing what you know now, what's the biggest mistake you see athletes make today in regard to their salaries and earnings?*

OSCAR: *Overspending! Creating a high overhead without a long-term plan to sustain it.*

DON: *What's the best piece of advice you received when you were making money during your career?*

OSCAR: *Leave the toy buying for the kids—no need to buy excess or unnecessary things.*

DON: *What's the best advice you would give to a young athlete coming into money?*

OSCAR: *When making one dollar, budget to 50 cents. The other half belongs to Uncle Sam.*

Oscar De La Hoya knows a thing or two about making a lot of money. It would have been easy for him to think that with the level of earnings he had, he'd never run out of money. But he knew better—and because of his wise decisions and his focus on SAVING rather than SPENDING, he is a wildly successful entrepreneur today.

3. POOR INVESTMENT CHOICES (AND DECISIONS)

There is a common idea that we grow wiser as we grow older. It's also true that, "We shall not grow wiser before we learn that much that we have done was very foolish."[14] Sometimes, we really do have to learn from our mistakes—and for professional athletes and their poor investment choices, this rings so very true. Unfortunately, the hard lessons come at a very high price for athletes, which can lead them in dire straits for the rest of their lives.

Most people make the lion's share of their financial mistakes and engage in foolish spending in their early years. As such, they are usually able to come back from them. They get older and wiser and become more disciplined savers and investors. In addition, most people's earnings increase over time during the course of their careers. The Traditional Income Path allows for a person to work 40 to 60 years, whereas a professional athlete's earnings window is microscopic in comparison, ranging from three to five years on average, 3 ½ to be exact.

As we discussed, this puts professional athletes on an Opposite Income Path, dooming them to make most of their money in their early years. Just because a professional athlete is young and rich, it doesn't mean they are gifted with good business sense, and that they make the best financial and mental choices for their own good. That's understandable—when you are young and impulsive. Aren't we all impulsive during our younger years? Some of us still are in our later years, too. The real problem is that when athletes make poor business and investment decisions, those decisions usually end up haunting them for the rest of their lives. Such bad decisions typically stem from their network of non-professionals which includes family members, friends, and sketchy so-called "advisors" that aren't advisors at all. They are just "takers" looking to exploit them. There are people who become leeches

---

14   Quote by Friedrich Hayek, economist and philosopher (1899–1992).

who will try to blow rainbows or smoke up their ass to make them feel good about investing in their shady schemes. So beware!

Many star athletes have lost millions of dollars in high-risk investments, despite the fact it's fairly common knowledge that hardly any (only one out of every thirty) high-risk private equities are successful. Most sound and reputable financial advisors would agree that you should put no more than ten percent of your liquid assets into high-risk investments. Well, those advisors certainly seem to have a hard time getting through to athletes who want to gamble with their money and invest in get-rich-quick schemes. Here are some documented cases where an athlete was not aware of the low probability of success for high-risk investments, got bad advice, or possibly just ignored their advisors because they were swinging for the fences:

Curt Schilling. One of the best pitchers of his era, Curt Schilling, who pitched in the World Series on a torn tendon in his ankle, ended his career in 2008. After he retired, he started looking for ways to make more money and invest what was left of his earnings. He went on to lose as much as $50 million in a video game company that he founded and started. Unfortunately, that was all the money that he had left after a twenty-year career in baseball. He even had to ask the Hall of Fame to return his bloody sock that he had worn when he pitched in the World Series on his torn tendons in his ankle so that he could auction it off for a little over $92,000. Luckily, he was able to work for ESPN for a few years, but unfortunately he got fired for expressing his controversial "politically incorrect" opinion.

Sheryl Swoopes. Sheryl was a WNBA star and MVP, a three-time Olympic medalist, and the first female basketball athlete to have her own shoe, the Nike Air Swoopes. She made over $50 million in her career, but because of a series of bad investments, and "shady" lawyers and agents, she filed for Chapter 13 bankruptcy in 2004. According to

Money Magazine, she was so poor that she was unable to pay her rent. Sadly, she also had to sell her Olympic medals to cover her debts.

Raghib Ismail. The "Rocket!" Raghib Ismail was arguably one of the most electrifying athletes to come out of college. He snubbed the NFL—where he probably would have been the number one draft pick—and signed with the CFL's Toronto Argonauts in 1991 for a guaranteed $18.2 million over four years. At the time, it was one of the richest contracts in football history. He then proceeded to make a series of high-risk investments that turned into bad investments. In 1991, he invested $300,000 into the Rock 'n Roll Cafe, a knockoff of the well-known Hard Rock Cafe, and he lost all his investment. He also put a small fortune into a movie and a music label, a cosmetic procedure where oxygen absorbs into the skin, and phone card dispensers. Even with all the hard lessons under his belt, he didn't stop. Ismail then invested $250,000 into a special mouth guard (an investment that actually seems to be a panning out). Fortunately for Ismail, he also has a degree from Notre Dame to fall back on. If only other players were so fortunate.

Antoine Walker. With an NBA career spanning twelve years, Antoine Walker made over $108 million in his basketball career. However, in addition to overspending, Antoine bought over 140 properties across Chicago just a few years before the most recent financial crisis. When the financial crisis hit in 2008, Antoine nearly lost everything and two years later filed for bankruptcy. Antoine said, "You never think about the future when you make that type of money. It's something that never crosses your mind."[15] This a good lesson to learn about stewardship, from what Antoine is saying. You want to be conscious of where your money is going.

---

15   Tandon, Shraysi. "Top-earning professional athletes go bankrupt from poor investments." Cctv.com. Jan 30, 2015. Web.

Marion Jones. She was once the All-American girl. Marion had the whole world in her hands with all her grace, beauty, and power. She was a track and field superstar, a WNBA star, and at one point, she was known as the fastest woman on the planet. She won three gold medals and two bronze medals in the Sydney Olympics. She also won three gold medals as a World Champion. At the height of her career, she was making over $7 million a year. But soon after, she lost everything after admitting to using steroids (the infamous Balco case), lying to a grand jury, and committing perjury to the IRS, and check counterfeiting and forging. She filed for bankruptcy claiming to only have $2,000 to her name.

Derrick Coleman. Born in Mobile, Alabama and raised in Detroit, Michigan. Derrick Coleman was the number one draft pick of the New Jersey Nets in 1990. In bankruptcy court, it was reported that Derrick Coleman had debts of $4.6 million and assets of about $1 million. He made many bad investments in various real estate deals and investments meant to help his bankrupt childhood hometown of Detroit.

Dorothy Hamill. She was one of the greatest ice skaters ever and a trendsetter of her time. At age nineteen, she won Olympic gold in Innsbruck, Austria. Even though she was an enormous underdog, she still pulled it off. She had that recognizable wedge haircut that almost every American girl wanted, thus landing her many lucrative endorsements and commercials for Clairol. She was the first woman to earn a $1 million contract for a female athlete when she signed with the Ice Capades. Hamill ended up buying the Ice Capades to revive the sport, which ended up being an unwise move (especially trying to compete with Disney on Ice). She ended up filing for bankruptcy and blamed her ex-husband for making many poor investment choices.

Torii Hunter. It's a bird! It's a plane! It's MLB star Torii Hunter leaping over the wall to rob a homerun from the opposition! Torii Hunter has made a fortune—over $172 million —leaping like superman and robbing homeruns. Hunter isn't bankrupt and hasn't reported any financial troubles since he is still playing and earning over $10 million a year, but he did talk about $70,000 that he lost in a bad investment on an inflatable raft. According to *Sports Illustrated*, "The pitch was that when high–rainfall areas were flooded, consumers could pump up the raft, allowing a sofa to float and remain dry." It sounds like a great idea in theory, but as Hunter discovered, most high-risk investments end up, well, sinking.

When you hear the name Bernard (Bernie) Madoff, most of us probably think of Ponzi schemes. Madoff received 150 years in prison for running the largest Ponzi scheme in history, conning investors out of over $65 billion over several decades. The name originated with Charles Ponzi, who once promised 50 percent returns on investments in only 90 days. Although Madoff made the Ponzi scheme famous, such fraudulent acts have actually been around since 1899. A Ponzi scheme is defined as:

A fraudulent investment operation where the operator, an individual or organization, pays returns to its investors from new capital paid to the operators by new investors, rather than from profit earned by the operator.

If you think Ponzi schemes are only for average or uneducated (but money hungry) investors, think again. Many famous athletes have been swindled by these illegal operations. Players like John Elway, Fred Taylor, Mike Pelfrey, Johnny Damon, and Jacoby Ellsbury among others have all been burned for a combined total of over a $100 million. The bottom line: ***Sometimes, when something sounds too good to be true, it almost always certainly is.***

I had the privilege of speaking with my friend and mentor, David Meltzer, CEO of Sports1Marketing, public speaker, and author of the bestselling book, *Connected to Goodness*. His newest book is *Compassionate Capitalism*. Before David co-founded Sports1Marketing with NFL

Hall of Fame great Warren Moon, David was CEO of the world's most recognized sports agency, Leigh Steinberg Sports and Entertainment. He has also been profiled by national publications such as *Forbes*, ESPN, CNBC, and Bloomberg. David Meltzer was recently honored by *Variety Magazine* and Unite4:Good Foundation as the Sports Humanitarian of the Year for his involvement with over 100 charitable events and foundations annually.

I asked David to tell me about the mistakes that he sees professional athletes making and what other options are available to athletes so they can make wise decisions. Here is what he had to say:

DON: *David, knowing what you know now, what's the biggest mistake you see athletes coming into money making today?*

DAVID: *Getting married while they play without a prenuptial agreement, having kids with more than one partner, and investing irresponsibly.*

DON: *What's the best piece of advice you received when you began making some serious money?*

DAVID: *Put half of your money into guaranteed annuities.*

DON: *What's the best advice you would give a young athlete coming into money who has never grown up with money and is having his whole world transformed?*

DAVID: *Put half of your money into annuities, have a prenuptial agreement, and only have kids with your wife. Don't invest in anything you don't know about. If a guy has a stem cell company, why is he coming to you and not someone that knows about it?*

DON: *What's next for David Meltzer and Sports1Marketing?*

DAVID: *For Sports1Marketing, I like to suggest using the website—www.processingforacause.com—that website and virtual gifting are the best two ways to make a lot of money, help a lot of people and have a lot of fun.*

For more information about David Meltzer check out his books and articles: *Way to Happiness, Getting Out of your Own Way, Compassionate Capitalism,* and *Trust the Universe but Tie Up Your Camels.* David also has a radio show on Yahoo Sports and ESPN with Jim Leyritz, and he has many speaking engagements where he empowers others to be happy!

Successful innovators like David recognize that life is more fulfilling when you make a difference in as many people's lives as possible. He only takes on clients and projects where a difference will also be made philanthropically. He learned this from Leigh Steinberg, where their agency would only take on clients that were willing to give back and somehow invest in their communities or charities. David knows that athletes have the unique opportunity to do so much good and have enormous impact socially and economically with their fame and wealth. When you do that, there is no telling how many people and causes you can help.

4. FAMILY PRESSURES

Athletes have it so easy, right? All they do is throw some form of ball around a few hours a week, and they make millions of dollars. They get to travel all over the world, have perks thrown at them, get their meals comped wherever they go, and have women waiting for them in every hotel lobby. While it's easy to make such blanket statements about athletes based on what we can see (and with no real knowledge of what it takes to play at the professional level). One thing that is undeniable is that having a lot of money makes the topic of *family* not so simple.

Professional athletes live their lives in a fishbowl. The public gets a front-row seat to some of their most intimate moments, greatest achievements, and their worst days and situations. A lot of the time, the price of this fame and front-and-center lifestyle is the erosion of personal relationships. For many wives, girlfriends, and children, it's more than they can take. Just about every person has a phone with a camera on it. Because of Facebook, Instagram, and the power of social media, we know when an athlete either cheats on his partner, files for divorce or is in some type of trouble—sometimes even before their partners do or they even know.

When it comes to family pressures, there is nobody more experienced in knowing what the modern athlete goes through than Harvard Trained Psychiatrist, Dr. Tim Benson, who specializes in working with successful individuals who perform or compete in high-stress environments.

I have had a great opportunity to get to know Dr. Tim and his family as we are in the process of completing a "Game Changer Program" for athletes called "Surviving Success, Mentally, Spiritually, and Financially," (for more information go to SSMSFacademy.com).

What makes Dr. Tim so special is: He was an All-American, scholar-athlete who pursued Sports Psychiatry in order to support athletes who are focused on achieving and sustaining their dreams while creating a legacy that benefits future generations. Not only does Dr. Tim have a big mission, he has served as a clinician for the NBA/NBPA Player Assistance and Anti-Drug Program. Currently, he works with the LA Rams as a coordinator for their Rookie Success Program. He provides mental performance coaching for college and professional athletes, and provides talks and workshops for athletic teams nationally.

DON: *Dr. Tim, I have known you a little over a year, and it's been a journey with moving from Boston to Los Angeles. Please tell us about the journey these young men and women go through and the process these athletes deal with when it comes to "Family Pressures?"*

DR. TIM: *The journey of an athlete who is thrust into the spotlight can be very difficult if there isn't a strong foundation. Oftentimes what you see is that many athletes assume that what got them there is what is going to keep them there. They feel that as long as they work hard on their craft they will be OK. This is far from the truth. There are other factors that now come into play that will be critical to ongoing success given the fact that as you ascend to higher levels there will be an increase in demands, expectations and competition. This all comes with elevated pressures. What an athlete has to learn quickly is how to ask for help and be open to new ways of growth. In order to prevent a career catastrophe, it is imperative that the athlete ensure that their personal growth keeps pace with their professional growth.*

DON: *I know you cannot disclose names, but can you explain a couple situations that many of these men and women go through?*

DR. TIM: *A common challenge at the professional level is handling the demands of friends and family. What most people don't realize is that the athlete not only has to deal with their own expectations of what it means to be successful, but they also have to manage the expectations of others. Family members are those who have known and supported them the longest before there was a spotlight. Therefore, it can be hard to say "no" to requests for money and favors. It is often out of a sense of guilt that causes the athlete to overextend themselves in order to give to others. If this occurs too frequently, athletes can get into debt quickly.*

DON: *What counsel can you give them when so many of their family members are coming after them for their time and resources?*

DR. TIM: *The best advice I can give them is to learn how to set boundaries early. Saying "no" doesn't mean that you don't love your family or that you are selfish. What it means is that before you make too many financial commitments there needs to be a strategy and structure in place. It is also important for athletes to know what it means to enable someone versus empower them. Enabling refers to any action that perpetuates the status quo. Empowering refers to actions that build a person's level of confidence and competence to make a significant change in their own situation. Constantly bailing someone out does not typically foster growth. Giving is great only if it is from a place of gratitude and not out of guilt. Setting boundaries is a part of a healthy self-respect that can eventually lead you to positions of influence that yield a greater and more sustaining impact.*

ATHLETES AND THE HIGH COST OF DIVORCE

Divorce—it's one of the ugliest words in the English dictionary. The word alone makes you feel like a failure or simply makes you cringe. Not only is a divorce one of the costliest things an athlete can experience financially, it is also one of the most mentally and spiritually draining experience any human being can go through. Here are a few examples of the high cost of divorce in the world of professional sports:[16]

Tiger Woods. The story of Tiger's rampant infidelity was front-page news in the media for a long time, as was the story of his enraged wife, now ex-wife, Elin, battering him with his own golf clubs. The divorce from the Swedish model cost Tiger over $100 million from his vast fortune. Perhaps even more substantial than that, he lost endorsement deals with several prominent companies in the wake of the scandal. In fact, according to *Forbes*, he now earns $54 million a year in endorsements, half of what he earned before the scandal. It's been over seven years since the scandal, and Tiger still hasn't regained his stature as the most dominant golfer ever.

---

16   Saito, Kevin. "Top 15 Most Expensive Divorces for Professional Athletes." *The Sportster*. Oct 7, 2014. Web.

Michael Jordan. The greatest basketball player of our time had it all. Unfortunately for his wife, that also meant he had his pick of women. Amid allegations of rampant infidelity, Jordan's wife, Juanita filed for divorce. In one of the most expensive divorces an athlete has ever had, Juanita slammed her soon-to-be ex with a $168 million settlement.

Shaquille O'Neal. Shaquille O'Neal is one of the greatest centers to ever play the game of basketball. By some estimates, over the course of his career, Shaq has made over $300 million in salary and endorsements. He's not hurting for money, but his accounts got a little bit lighter when his wife, Shaunie filed for divorce, claiming rampant infidelity. A detailed account of the settlement wasn't released publicly, but it has been reported that Shaq is paying her at least $20,000 a month in alimony (and that doesn't include the likely hefty settlement payout).

Divorce is almost never a good thing for families. It separates children from their parents, and in most athletes' cases, it means that they rarely see their kids. The majority of divorce cases award primary custody to the mother. Children become more susceptible to behavioral issues, bad performance in school, involvement with drugs and alcohol, as well as sexual intercourse more so than those children and teens from families that stay together. As glamorous as being a professional athlete may seem to some, the financial and emotional toll it can take on the athlete and his family often outweighs the appeal. What's the point of success if your family and/or your kids are jacked up? Is that truly success or happiness?

5. ALLOWING THE WRONG PEOPLE INTO YOUR INNER CIRCLE

If you're broke, you can be certain that your friends (and even your family) don't just hang around you for your money—and there's some peace in that fact. When you are wealthy—and especially in the cases where the wealth comes on fast—old "friends" and maybe even some long-lost family members will come out of the woodwork to become "a special and meaningful part of your life." Professional athletes have to contend with a variety of leeches (for lack of a better term) once that first signing bonus rolls in—and it only gets worse from there. For players who aren't prepared for the onslaught of new and old friends, it can be tempting to divvy out a little money here and there to such people. The problem is, over time, those little "loans" here and there can really add up. There is no room in your circle for leeches, but whom can you trust? It's a tough—and often expensive—question to answer.

THE "CURSE" OF PROFESSIONAL SPORTS?

There is a phenomenon you may have heard about known as the "Lottery Curse." The "curse" of the lottery refers to the supposed bad luck that a sudden large influx of money brings to a person. Here are two prime examples:

- David Edwards won $27 million in a Powerball jackpot, and spent much of it on drugs, a mansion, a Lear jet, and fancy new cars. With $27 million, you could live comfortably for the rest of your life without working; but Edwards spent lavishly, and ended up living in a filthy storage unit late in his life. His wife eventually left him and he died in hospice care.
- Billie Bob Harrell, Jr. won $31 million in the Texas Lotto in 1997. He enjoyed his new wealth at first, quitting his job, taking his family to Hawaii, donating money to his church, and buying cars and houses for friends and relatives. But soon, people he knew and some he didn't know were hitting him up for money. He made some bad business decisions, and his wife left him. Ultimately, he was found dead of a gunshot wound. He reportedly told a financial advisor, "Winning the lottery is the worst thing that ever happened to me."

Professional athletes can relate all too well to these woes. It seems that the lottery and the world of professional sports have something in common. Getting a large sum of money all at once causes a flood of temptations to rain down upon you from every possible angle.

- Athletes want the new cars and the big house.
- They want to buy or pay off their mom's house.
- They want to buy their girlfriend a Ferrari or a "big rock."
- They want to see the world.
- Their friends and family need a loan (that they never intend to pay back).
- Would-be inventors and others seek start-up capital for a "sure thing."

In short, everyone around you wants a piece of your large—but ultimately fleeting—pie. What is the solution? The answer isn't to cut yourself off from society, stick your money under the mattress, eat Top Ramen noodles, and shop only at Wal-Mart. *There is a way to enjoy your life <u>while</u> you make sound financial choices—and the answers lie in the pages ahead.*

Don't walk through life just playing football. Don't walk through life just being an athlete. Athletics will fade. Character and integrity and really making an impact on someone's life, that's the ultimate vision, that's the ultimate goal - bottom line.

—RAY LEWIS

2

The Psychology, Flow, and Soul of Money

—

IS IT REALLY ABOUT THE MONEY?

Country music legend Winona Judd has a similar past to that of many professional athletes today. She grew up poor, but by the age of 17, she had become a megastar with gold and platinum records and international stardom. Money was being hurled at her in every direction. But, after amassing a fortune, she squandered much of it, throwing money at her children out of guilt for missing their games and recitals, and buying more cars than she could ever drive.

Years later, she ended up in rehab—but not the kind that is featured on shows like *Intervention* or that spoiled celebs go to after a weeklong bender in Vegas. No, she went to *money rehab*, where, in six days of group therapy they dug deep into the roots of what psychologists call *money disorders*—the slew of unhealthy and self-destructive behaviors that are seemingly not as extreme as pathological gambling, kleptomania or compulsive shopping, but nevertheless afflict large numbers of people.[17]

Money disorders are not universally recognized and not even very publicized, and yet they afflict untold numbers. Experts in psychology and financial planning say the number of professionals offering to treat money disorders has multiplied in the last few years—and for good reason. Although there are countless self-help books on how to *become rich*, the fields of psychology and financial planning have been slow to link money with *emotion*. In fact, money is still a great cultural taboo that is rarely discussed openly in this country.

This reveals that money habits and problems are a whole lot more than what we see on the surface—and no one is all that interested in digging in deeper to find out from where these issues stem. It also explains why all those "how to get rich" books leave out a very important detail—and that is how to <u>stay</u> rich and fulfilled at the same time.

THE ROOT OF OUR MONEY BELIEFS

What's goin' on? What's goin' on?
I don't know what they want from me.
It's like the more money we come across,
The more problems we see.

Those are lyrics from the song "Mo Money, Mo Problems" by the late Notorious B-I-G. This was Christopher Wallace's (aka Biggie Smalls) mindset about money, and it seems that most Americans can

---

17 Klontz, Brad. Do You Have a Money Disorder?" *Psychology Today*. January 30, 2010.

relate. Just about everyone has a complicated relationship with money. Studies show that money is the number one reason for divorce in the early years of marriage and a common area of conflict for couples. Even before the most recent recession, three out of four Americans identified money as the number one source of stress in their lives.[18]

At a time when the economy is stagnating and consumers are fearful about unemployment and retirement savings, it is easy to imagine that being rich like a professional athlete or movie star, or coming upon some sort of windfall, is a *panacea*—a cure-all—and that anyone who has money must surely feel so secure and serene. ***But plenty of people struggling with money issues are _not_ poor.*** Research has shown a significant level of depression, for example, among lottery winners. Other research has shown that above a household income of $50,000, there is little or no correlation between income and happiness.[19]

This all begs the question: *Why do we do it?* Why do professional athletes and others who become rich spend their money faster than they make it? If "common sense" tells us that money is liquid, and that spending more than you make will lead to having less money, then why does this problem persist?

It's because *common sense* has very little to do with it.

The "psychology of money" is multilayered and mysterious, and it goes far beyond our conscious thought and deep into our subconscious. According to licensed clinical psychologist Dr. James Gottfurcht:

The psychology of money is how our beliefs, expectations, and feelings influence our financial behavior, success, and disappointment. This means that financial

---

18   Kershaw, Sarah. "How to treat a 'money disorder'." *The New York Times*, Accessed October 19, 2015. Web.

19   Gregoire, Carolyn. "How Money Changes The Way We Think And Behave." *The Huffington Post*, January 23, 2014.

success is an 'inside job' and is more determined by what's between our ears and inside our hearts than what's on the outside.

Dr. Gottfurcht says that even though the *psychology of money* emphasizes how our brains process thoughts and actions related to money, the same mindset that creates (or destroys) financial success also creates (or destroys) success in our relationships, careers, health, and lifestyle. In short, it is your inner world—and not the dollar amount in your bank account—that creates your outer world.

How you spend your money, then, has little to do with your taste in cars, clothes, homes, parties, or exotic destinations, and a whole lot more to do with what you have been taught, either consciously or subconsciously, about money over the years.

Thanks to what we were taught or simply witnessed during our childhood and teenage years, many of us grow up thinking that money is a "necessary evil." We all want more of it, but we also believe somewhere in our minds (and we may not even realize it) that, as Biggie said, "The more money we come across, the more problems we see."

CONFRONTING YOUR INNER WORLD

People are more focused on the *problems* with money rather than what the real problem is, and here's a little secret for you—that problem has nothing to do with money. T. Harv Eker said in his book, *Secrets of the Millionaire Mind*:

...people will do almost anything to avoid problems. They see a challenge and they run...the secret to success, my friends, is not to try to avoid or get rid

of or shrink from your problems; the secret is to grow yourself so that you are bigger than your problems.

What that means for you is this: The more *you* grow, the more your income will grow. We can even take it a step further as an athlete to say that the better and more skilled you become, the bigger your contract will be. I didn't understand this concept until I started on a path toward my own personal growth over the past several years. Although looking within yourself can be confronting, especially when it means exposing your open wounds, scars and skeletons, it will feel like you've been given a new lease on life when you successfully move past all of that baggage. Personal growth will lead you toward more fulfilling relationships, not only with others but with yourself—and a by-product of that is a happier and more fulfilling life.

The good news is, if there's one group of individuals who understand the concept of "no pain, no gain," it is professional athletes. Think of the countless hours you've spent becoming part of an elite group of players that the whole world admires. You already know what it takes to get to the top of the athletic game. Well, the same effort is required to stay at the top of the *money game*. If you want to acquire more wealth and actually keep it and grow it, it's absolutely essential to get rid of the "demons" of your past that come in many forms.

Maybe you don't even know what those demons are—and that's okay. They aren't always obvious, which is what makes ridding ourselves of them so hard. Our brains are these truly amazing machines. They have the ability to take a memory and morph it into a whole other reality. They can mask painful times in our past so that we can go on living without constant reminders. The brain also has the capacity to store almost every last thing you see and hear—and all of that becomes your "subconscious." And here's the thing; just because you don't dwell on the past or think about the money lessons (or lack thereof) you learned, doesn't mean your brain didn't tuck it away somewhere for safekeeping, and it certainly doesn't mean you aren't affected or even scarred by those things.

Personal growth requires you to "dig in" and discover what really makes you tick. People who open themselves up for the first time are often surprised by the hidden motivating factors that have been subconsciously steering the ship. It can be daunting—but it can also be one of the most freeing processes you will ever experience.

HIDDEN HAPPINESS VAMPIRES

Another factor that can make personal growth a challenge is the people around us. After I started taking conscious steps toward personal growth, most of the people I grew up with laughed at me and called me a sellout for deviating from "the way things have always been" and for trying to find a better and more satisfied life for myself. That really just proves one universal truth:

There are your real friends—and then there's everyone else.

For most of us, the real friends and supporters are few and far between. One of the hardest things I ever did in my life was to separate myself from some of the people I grew up with, but it was necessary for my own health and happiness. As Jim Rohn says, "You are the average of the five people you spend the most time with." While that doesn't take into account your own conscious choices, the point is that who you spend time with influences the person you eventually become. *That also means that those around you can either elevate you or bring you down.*

We've all had those people in our lives who brighten a room when they come in, and we've all probably experienced people who can brighten a room by *leaving* it. Each one of us has our own energy, thoughts, and beliefs that shape who we are, and, depending on who we choose to surround ourselves with, those things will either elevate us toward greater success or lead us down a path to fewer successes—and ultimately less fulfillment.

The type of people you interact with influences the consciousness level you operate in as well as your habits and actions. These people don't necessarily "change" you—they merely bring out a side of you that is already there. In short, the people around you have far more power over your life than you could ever possibly realize. You may be the most conscientious and smartest individual around, but if you are constantly surrounded by negative, fear-based people, those vibes will tap into any pessimism and fear inside of you (that maybe you weren't even aware of), and it will have an impact on who you eventually become and your progression in life.

WHAT MONEY REPRESENTS

One of the biggest revelations of my adult life took place during a self-growth course by Landmark Education, and it was this: *The more money I made, the more important I felt.* It was the first time I realized that dollar bills and bank account balances represented so much more than numbers to me. I didn't realize I was actually basing my self-worth on how much money I made rather than on my core values—and maybe I didn't even know what those core values really were or what my purpose was.

As a result, I had also been treating others based on their net worth and not their hearts. It's often been said that the way you treat service people—like waiters or housekeepers—reveals your hidden true character. I remember treating an ex-girlfriend poorly. I wasn't consistent in my affection and attention toward her because she had less money than I did and I felt she didn't contribute to the "bottom line." At the time, of course, it didn't dawn on me why I didn't treat her the way she deserved to be treated. I would even talk down to her, saying things to put her in her place like, "I rescued you from the hood. You are lucky to be with me." Not very nice, I'll admit.

It wasn't until years later, after that weekend course, that I realized the problem wasn't her—I was the one with the problem. I reached out to her after the course and apologized for the way I had treated her and asked her for her forgiveness. There is no one on this earth who is more valuable than the person next to him or her. We are all the same—we're all human beings who want to love, want to be loved, and desire security and happiness. I would probably not be married today with my beautiful wife and children next to me if it weren't for this realization.

THE SILENT DICTATOR OF OUR LIVES

Our subconscious is wreaking havoc on our lives and our finances. The problem is, because it is your *subconscious*, which is defined as "the part of the mind of which one is not fully aware but which influences one's actions and feelings," we live our lives unaware of the real culprit of our money disorders and of our endless pursuit of the wrong things. It's possible to avoid the pitfalls of your subconscious if you are willing and able to develop your awareness of your underlying messages and beliefs about self-worth and money.

Your subconscious is your inner world that will determine your outer world, and whatever situation you are in now is a reflection of your thoughts, feelings, and emotions. Here is a question you may have never thought about: *What are your past experiences with money from childhood?* Maybe your parents said things like, "I work hard for my money!" or "We'll never be able to afford that!" or "You can't take it with you!" Whatever you heard—guess what? It stuck with you, and it's playing a significant and powerful role in your current money mindset. To discover the root of your feelings about and actions with money, let's dig into your past a little.

Write down your memories of childhood conversations with your parents or other influencers about money.

_____

_____

_____

_____

_____

Write down how you think these conversations have affected your adult life.

_____

_____

_____

_____

_____

I remember listening to my mom and first stepdad argue over money all the time. One day, they got in a huge argument about the fact that my stepdad was saving too much money in his personal account and not in the family account (since everything was supposed to be shared 50/50). I was eleven years old at the time, so that didn't even register with me, right? Wrong. Let's fast-forward eighteen years later to when I got married. When we got back from our three-week honeymoon in Europe, my wife said, "Let's combine everything." My kneejerk response was, "OH, HELL NO! We are going to have separate accounts."

In my mind, I felt this was necessary in order to ensure that we didn't fight about money. *How ironic.* My wife was extremely hurt by my reaction because of her wholly different family experience with money. When she was growing up, everything was shared, through thick and thin. In her head, my intention to keep "my money" away from "her money" signified that we were already separating just after getting married. She saw it as me keeping one foot out the door, just in case. These disparate views on money put a huge strain on our marriage, and just one week after our honeymoon, resentment had started to grow.

Luckily, I came to my senses and willingly shared my income into our joint account with her income. Think about how many marriages end because of issues like this—issues that have little or nothing to do with the two people who fell in love. They are issues that stem from our childhoods that are lying dormant in our subconscious, just waiting to surface and wreak havoc.

What did (or didn't) your parents teach you about money? How is that affecting the way you treat "your" money today?

A LESSON IN SELF-SABOTAGE

Nobody ever sat me down and taught me *anything* about money, and it certainly showed. My first job in seventh grade was delivering newspapers. It required me to collect the money, pay the newspaper company a certain percentage of what I collected, and keep the rest. Because I knew nothing about money, I just did what "felt right." I'd overspend on ice cream and always get behind paying the newspaper company their share. Eventually, I was fired. I didn't have the discipline to sacrifice *now* for the payoff *later*, nor did I know how to save. That was the beginning of a long journey of "monetary self-sabotage" for me. Dr. Mamiko Odegard, an authority on avoiding and overcoming self-sabotage so you can have love, happiness, and financial success, describes self-sabotage this way:

> *To consciously or unconsciously make moment-to-moment decisions that lead to self-defeat, regret, frustration, anger, low esteem, a sense of failure and feelings of being trapped and stuck.*

Self-sabotage can be chronic, becoming automatic in the ways you deny yourself rewards and goals—while shortchanging yourself and leaving you feeling worthless and dissatisfied. It is expressed daily in the choices you make. No one wakes up in the morning hell-bent on sabotaging his or her finances, and yet it happens all the time. This just proves the fact that much of our actions and beliefs stem from our subconscious.

What does money really mean to you? If you have a lot, do you feel accomplished, successful, or worthy? If you have a little or none, are you sad or depressed? Does the amount in your bank account have any bearing on your self-worth?

_____

_____

_____

_____

_____

Before I realized that *internal well-being* is what makes you happy, I used to think if I had money and possessions, I'd be happy. I thought the "things" were what really mattered. Back in high school, my Aunt Yoli helped me buy a Ninja 250 motorcycle. At that moment, I believed I was the coolest teenager on the planet because I had a job that paid me money, which made me feel independent and invincible, and I had an outward sign of that money—a cool motorcycle. It took years of working hard to pay for that bike. I even had to miss some of the most important events and milestones in high school working overtime to make the payments. At the end of it all, the bike eventually got stolen. What a waste of time and what misplaced priorities.

THE ROOT OF ALL EVIL?

Mark Kinney said it best when it described money like this: "Money is like an iron ring we put through our nose. It is now leading us around wherever it wants. We just forgot that we are the ones who designed it." Money only has the power that we give it, and in America and many parts of the world, we have given it enormous power—far more power than it deserves. We have given it more value than we place on human lives. As a species, we have killed for it, enslaved people for it, and we have enslaved ourselves to depressing lives in the pursuit of it.

In some parts of the world, children are forced to have an eye gouged out with a hot iron rod or a body part cut off so they can get more sympathy (and thus more money) as they beg on street corners, a horrible truth that was depicted in the movie *Slumdog Millionaire*. We have also done massive damage to our planet; destroying rain forests, damming and destroying rivers, cutting down forests, overfishing oceans and rivers, and putting poisons into our soil and water. These are some of the behaviors that have really set us back as a society, and they all stem from one thing—the pursuit of the almighty dollar. This, of course, is the reason why people have dubbed money as the "root of all evil." But is it, really? The bottom line is this:

Money isn't evil; it's the behavior behind the money that's evil. The behavior is the key, not the money—and behavior will also dictate whether you will find and hold on to success in your relationships, career, health, and lifestyle.

I would also agree with the King James Bible, 1 Timothy 6:10 reads, "For the love of money is the root of all evil: which while some coveted after, they have erred from the faith, and pierced themselves through with many sorrows."

Money isn't evil—but it's also not just "a means to an end." It can and should mean so much more, but not because of what it can buy; it's because of what it can do. In America, every choice (from the most life-changing choices to everyday decisions) we make depends on it. Here are just a few examples. Money determines:

- The food we consume
- The clothes we wear
- The education we receive
- The careers we choose
- The kind of wedding we have
- The people who call themselves our "friends"
- The home we live in
- The number of children we have
- The age at which we can retire

The list could go on and on. Almost every decision we make is dependent upon the amount of money we have or are willing to spend. One of the biggest decisions I made was opting for community college before I went to a university because I couldn't afford a larger school. When I transferred to California State University, Northridge I was still close enough to commute back and forth from my grandmother's house. Looking back, I realize that I never really got the "college experience" of living in a dorm or being on my own in college. My wife says she learned so much from living with six random roommates, and it helped her better manage her life and her budget. She also says she discovered who she was as an individual after she stepped out on her own, away from the major influencing forces of her childhood.

Money is power, actually it is not. Knowledge is power, as one of my mentors Armand Morin says in his pre-released book Success Leaves Traces: "Money is NOT power. Knowledge is power. Specific knowledge. You can have all the money in the world, but if you do not have the knowledge of what to do with it, you'll soon be broke again."

What is the most important decision that you ever had to make that was contingent on the amount of money you had or were willing to spend? How is that decision still affecting you today?

_____

_____

_____

_____

FINDING A STRONG ENOUGH "WHY"

In my younger years, my mom made a choice between my stepfather and me. He didn't want me living with them anymore, and she chose him over me. I perceived it to be because he brought home a paycheck every two weeks. What that meant to me was that money was more important than I was. I felt like a nobody. I felt worthless and unloved. That's when I determined that, "Money is Power." or so I thought it was. A switch had flipped, and I decided I was going to be a millionaire so that I would not have to depend on anyone. I never again wanted to experience the horrible pain of rejection and abandonment. I was never going to allow anyone to choose between family and money. I wanted the power. Unfortunately, I took it a step further, and my pursuit of money took priority over emotional attachment.

It really could have gone either way for me. My family always lived paycheck to paycheck (and they didn't even do that very well). For many of us who grow up in that environment, we end up repeating the same life cycles also known as patterns. However, what stuck with me from that experience was the fact that, when given a choice, my mother chose money over her son—and that selfish choice spurred my commitment to become rich. *It became my "why" for being wealthy.* I was never going to be financially dependent on another person and be so vulnerable again.

Now, here's the funny (or not so funny) thing about that: When I started making a lot of money, do you think I was happy? I had the best cars, finest clothes, and beautiful women by my side. I traveled to the most desirable destinations on earth and got treated like royalty. I still wasn't happy. My *why* to be rich simply wasn't enough of a driving force. There was no "end game." There was no real purpose to my becoming rich. It was all about me, myself, and I. It was all so…empty.

What I had failed to realize in my subconscious was that the money had become a Band-Aid for wounds that needed real, substantial, and painful treatment and or healing. The money could never make me feel complete or worthwhile. Money can't do that for any of us, which leads us to you.

Why did you become an athlete? What does it mean to be an athlete? Do you want to be a role model? Is the prestige a burden? Do you live for the fame and glory? Do you think it's all about the money? Or maybe all of the above?

What's your internal dialogue about money? Does it mean power, freedom, security, worry, guilt, anger, sadness, happiness, love, or joy? Which words come to mind?

_____

_____

_____

_____

_____

WEALTH IS NOT ABOUT THE MONEY

The first step toward living the lifestyle you want, while at the same time, not allowing the money and the material things to consume you is to realize what the "real flow of money" looks like, and I'm not talking about: 1) Getting your paycheck, 2) Depositing it, and 3) Then either spending it or saving it. The flow of money is far deeper and more substantial than that. Do you know how money really flows to you and from you? Here is a simple diagram to demonstrate:

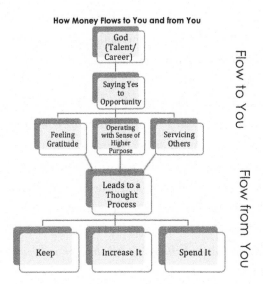

How Money Flows to You and from You

Wasn't expecting that? That's because the real and meaningful "flow of money" isn't about the money at all—and it has nothing to do with how talented you are, how sophisticated your taste is, or any other selfish factor. The underlying flow of money is about recognizing that you have a responsibility to recognize the real source of your money, and then seize opportunities to make it count for something in this world that extends far beyond your tiny bubble of existence.

There's a good chance that your own diagram doesn't look like this, or at least you don't believe it does. Maybe right now your money is going to cars and jewelry, or maybe you are making sound investments but still have fear and apprehension about your monetary future. Without a big enough WHY and without the right purpose in mind, no amount of spending or saving will get you where you want to be in life.

If you don't like what you see, you have the power and ability to change it and align your life and spending habits with your goals and values.

Lynne Twist said it best in one of the most profound books I have ever read, "*The Soul of Money*." She said, "Money travels everywhere, crosses all boundaries, languages, and cultures. Money, like water, ripples at some level through every life and place. It can carry our love or our fear. It can flood some of us such that we drown in a toxic sense of power over others. It can nourish and water the principles of freedom, community, and sharing. Money can affirm life or it can be used to demean, diminish, or destroy it. It is neither evil nor good; it is an instrument. We invented it, and it belongs squarely in the human experience, but it can be used by and merged with the longings and passions of our soul."

The first step toward changing a behavior is becoming <u>aware</u> of that behavior.

How do you currently decide how or when to spend money? What's your WHY or PURPOSE?

_____

_____

_____

_____

_____

What's your ultimate vision for your money?

_____

_____

_____

_____

_____

Do you feel grateful for the money you have earned or acquired? Why or why not?

_____

_____

_____

_____

_____

Consider this book and the questions I have asked you to be the beginning of your own "money rehab." You can change your future, regardless of the effect of the past on your subconscious. But, the key is this: You have to *consciously choose* to dig into the part of your mind that you have ignored or were not even aware existed—and that is when the healing process can begin.

I'm an athlete and I'm black, and a lot of black athletes go broke. I do not want to become a statistic, so maybe I overcompensate. But I'm paranoid. Oprah told me a long time ago, "You sign every check. Never let anyone sign any checks."

—SERENA WILLIAMS

3

Know Your Finances

—

Close your eyes and remember your first professional game or match. Do you remember that feeling of your heart pumping out of your chest? Maybe you couldn't tell if you were feeling excited, nervous, sick, making a huge mistake, or all of the above. Some athletes grow out of the pre-game jitters. Some don't. They say that NBA Boston Celtics great Bill Russell used to throw up before every one of his games.

For many elite athletes, that uncomfortable feeling before show time becomes the norm. In essence, they *become comfortable being uncomfortable*—which eventually makes them comfortable and helps them get in the zone. And that's when you realize that being uncomfortable may not be such a bad thing. In fact, that feeling of "being uncomfortable" really just means you are growing. You are not allowing your mind or body to accept status quo; you expect them both to grow, evolve, and improve.

You didn't get to where you are today professionally by avoiding those sometimes painful moments of growth and often-intense feelings of discomfort. You had to get to know your own body, test its limits on a daily basis, and allow it—and sometimes force it—to become the very best version of itself.

Why, then, would you expect real financial freedom and true solvency to come by chance? Far too many professional athletes learn the hard way that just because they make a large sum of money one year or even over the course of a few years doesn't mean they will become rich or stay rich. In fact, without taking the time to get to know your finances and learn how the process works, your bank account and your financial future will go from *being on the starting lineup* to *sitting it out on the bench* before you even know what hit you.

It may sound intimidating to "learn" about your finances, but it doesn't have to be hard. In fact, it's a lot easier to learn your finances now versus trying to learn them when you are "another broke athlete." You'll not only have to learn about your finances, you'll also need to learn how to rebuild your finances, which can be a more daunting and painful experience. In time, you'll learn your finances just like when you were first learning your sport. Tennis players, for example, don't expect to become experts at the serve, their groundstrokes, and the volley all at once. Instead, what do they do? They tackle each skill at a time. That is exactly what we are going to do with our discussion. We are going to dissect it in the same way you answer the question, "How do you eat an elephant?" *One bite at a time.* In this case, we are going to get to know your finances in three distinct parts:

1. Allocate your income.
2. Create a budget.

3. Manage cash flow.

We will go over each part in greater detail, starting with the most important first step, allocating your income in order to create a realistic budget.

PART I: ALLOCATE YOUR INCOME

How much should I spend each month? It's a question that can have many answers and depends on a great many variables. According to the U.S. Department of Labor and the U.S. Bureau of Labor statistics, the average American in 2010 spent $1,403 a month on housing, $639 a month on transportation, and $531 on groceries and dining. If only the government's spending were so simple. In 2015, the U.S. Government took in over $2 trillion, and they spent $3.9 trillion (see the chart below for a breakdown of U.S. Government spending).

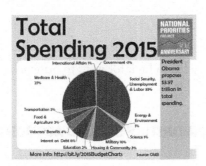

Sadly, most Americans operate at about 110 percent of their income, but unlike the U.S. Government, we can't just print more money to make up for the deficit. If we do, we will end up in prison. So, what can we do? A good foundation to follow is the 50/20/30 rule. Of course, like all financial plans, this must be altered to fit your specific financial situation, but it will provide you with an excellent starting point. The 50/20/30 rule breaks everything in your life that costs money down into three main categories, which are: 1) Essential Expenses, 2) Financial Priorities, and 3) Lifestyle Choices.

1. ESSENTIAL EXPENSES SHOULD ACCOUNT FOR 50 PERCENT.

Fifty percent or less of your net pay should go toward the essentials of everyday living, which include:

- Housing
- Utilities
- Groceries
- Insurance
- Tuition
- Charity
- Contractually obligated payments (like child support or alimony).

If you find that you already exceed the 50 percent mark spending on the essentials, you need to look for ways to bring that percentage down right away.

2. FINANCIAL PRIORITIES SHOULD ACCOUNT FOR 20 PERCENT.

Twenty percent of your income should be allocated to financial priorities that will increase your overall financial health. This money (or savings) include:

1. A "rainy day fund" that is comprised of at least nine to twelve months of your expenses in cash
2. Retirement savings

3. Big expenditure goals to save for like buying a house, college funding, or a future wedding

4. Debt repayments above the monthly minimum

3. LIFESTYLE CHOICES SHOULD ACCOUNT FOR 30 PERCENT.

When you allocate correctly, a third of your income can be set aside for lifestyle choices (i.e. your wants). This could include:

- Personal care
- Dining at restaurants
- Entertainment
- Sports and recreation
- Going to the movies
- Hobbies
- Private schooling and college
- Charity (charity can also be considered an essential expense depending on your personal and religious beliefs which includes the 10% tithe)

If you take care of your foundation first by maintaining a proportionate level of spending on both the essentials and financial priorities, you should never feel guilty about your spending in your lifestyle choices.

PART II: CREATE A BUDGET

Before you can really begin planning for your future, you've got to know how much money you need to maintain a comfortable, reasonable lifestyle while still enjoying all that life has to offer. That is why the critical next step in the process is to create a budget. In Budgeting 101, there are five simple steps:

1. Define your goals.
2. Determine where your income is coming from (from STEP 1).
3. Determine where your money is going.
4. Determine whether you have a surplus (more money coming in than out) or a deficit (more money going out than in).
5. Make adjustments when needed.

The first step in making a budget is to set goals. You may have heard of a commonly used acronym in business known as **S.M.A.R.T.** goals, with the letters in SMART standing for: *Specific, Measurable, Attainable, Realistic* and *Time-Based*:

Specific. Your goals must always be specific. How is this for a goal? *I want to be a good athlete.* That's a nice thought, but it is not specific enough. It's too vague—and the words "vague" and "goal" don't get along well together. How about this one? *I'd like to be debt free in three years.* That's more specific, and there are real steps that you can visualize to get you there.

Measurable. You've decided on a specific goal, and now it needs to be measurable. How about this goal? *I want to be rich.* While it's good to want to make more money by doing what you love and provide for your family, the best goals are measurable. This means you must establish concrete criteria for measuring your progress in attaining the goal. When you have a way to measure your progress, it makes it easier to stay on track and reach your target by a specific date.

Attainable. Once you have figured out what goals are most important to you, you must figure out ways to make them come true. When you see the way to the finish line, that's when you start to develop the attitude, skill, ability, and financial capacity to get you there. You can also begin to identify some of your previously overlooked opportunities and even discover ways you can reach your goal faster.

Realistic. In order for it to be realistic, a goal must represent an objective toward which you are both willing and able to work. A goal can be both <u>bold</u> and <u>realistic</u>, but you are the only one who can decide just how bold your goal should be. What does an unrealistic goal look like? It differs for everyone. You have to factor in your physical or financial situation, and then take it one day at a time.

Time-Based. The best goals are grounded with a time frame. With no time frame tied to something, there's no sense of urgency. "Someday" won't work. The best time frames are specific and give you a realistic platform on which to base your plan.

Now that you know each piece of a SMART goal, let's take it further with an example:

SMART GOAL EXAMPLE

Specific: I want to buy my dream house in two years.

Measurable: I need $200,000 as a down payment.

Attainable: I need to save $200,000/24 months = $8,334 per month.

Realistic: My goal is realistic based on my current salary of $1 million per year. After taxes (loosely estimated per year at $350,000) and current expenses ($15,000 per month), I can realistically save $8,334 per month for my new home and still set aside around $4,000 per month in savings.

Time-Based: I plan to reach this goal in two years.

What are your financial goals? What bills or debt do you want to pay off? Are you trying to save for a house, car, vacation, or retirement? You can have short-term (less than one year), mid-term (one to three years) and long-term goals (five or more years).

The first few times you sit down to determine your goals, it may seem like a daunting task. But the good news is that it does get much easier with practice. Go to www.notanotherbrokeathlete.com for a complimentary copy of the budget and SMART Goals worksheet.

Next, in order to turn your goals into reality, you will need to track your *inflows*—which is your cash coming in—and your *outflows* or expenses. You will know exactly how much money you need to come in to keep your lifestyle. Month by month, you can copy the worksheet so you are always aware if you are at a surplus or a deficit. You can also buy *Quicken*™, which is financial software that imports your bank and credit card transactions and uses them to help you see where you are and where you are headed. You, your Certified Public Accountant (CPA), or your Personal Assistant (PA) can import and categorize your transactions. This will show you exactly where you are spending your money.

IMPORTANT NOTE:

If you aren't the one tracking this information, make sure the person in charge of this reviews the numbers each month with you so you know exactly what is going on.

Nobody will or should care about your finances as much as you do. By knowing and committing these numbers to paper or in digital format (that you view on a consistent basis), you increase your chances of succeeding financially because you are anticipating future needs and know exactly how much money is flowing in and out. This will also help you spot issues before it's too late, since you may discover that you do not have enough money for emergencies, like a season-ending injury, a strike or lockout, or even a career change. Then, you can use this information to adjust your plans and expectations going forward.

A twelve-month budget can be updated with your actual expenses and the amount of income coming in each month so you will know whether you are on-target or off-target. If you are missing your targets in your budget, you can figure out how you can lower your expenses or increase your income, or both. These steps will keep your dream lifestyle a reality for the rest of your life.

KEY ASPECTS OF EVERY BUDGET

There are certain fundamental elements that every person must include in his or her budget. On the most basic level, you must know and be able to accurately track your income and your expenses, and then determine month by month whether you are at a surplus or deficit (i.e. Are you spending more than you are bringing in?). An easy place to start is by looking at last year's or even the last month's income and expenses, and then figuring out which numbers in the inflows and outflows will reoccur monthly.

When it comes to expenses, they are broken down into two categories:

1. *Fixed costs* are those expenses that remain mostly the same no matter the month or period. Some examples of fixed costs are:
   - Mortgage or rent
   - Property taxes
   - Food
   - Utilities
   - Lease or car payments
   - Debt payments
   - School tuition
   - Insurance premiums
   - Contributions to charity and/or tithe

2. *Variable costs*, however, tend to fluctuate from month to month and season to season. Some examples are:
   - Personal care

- Dining at restaurants
- Vacations
- Entertainment
- Sports and recreation
  - Going to the movies
  - Hobbies like golfing
  - Parties, clubs, bar tabs
  - Children's school and activities

MONEY BUCKETS

To make this process a little simpler, here is an exercise that may help. Consider your money fitting into three different buckets: Short-term money, mid-term money, and long-term money. Short-term money is comprised of the assets you are going to use within twelve months. It is your "everyday" money. Mid-term money is made up of expenses and goals that extend out three or so years (like saving for a house or college tuition). Long-term money is money that you will need five or more years in the future. This is also the money that is going to last you for the rest of your life (including the money you will use during your retirement years).

By placing your money needs in these three buckets, you will begin to more easily see if you have more money coming in or going out. You can now make adjustments in either direction. If you have a *surplus*, congratulations! You will be able spend a little more on some fancy toys, and/or you'll be able save for yours and your family's financial future. If you are at a *deficit*, you will need to figure out a way to make more money or spend less. ***It's difficult—and takes a huge commitment—to spend less.*** But it is possible. It will require you to analyze your expenses and break them down into "needs" versus "wants."

NEEDS VERSUS WANTS

Both fixed and variable expenses can be categorized as needs and wants. Typical needs are always going to include housing and food—since you need somewhere to live, and you have to eat. Other needs will also include anything that is necessary for your well-being and your dependents well-being. Wants, on the other hand, are things that are not necessary to live a healthy life with a roof over your head. But that doesn't mean you should or need to live without them. In most cases, it's both healthy and natural to have a mix of wants along with needs in your budget.

In my twenties, I was living paycheck-to-paycheck, despite the fact that I was making six figures a year. I had no budget and engaged in no planning or forecasting into the future. If I had extra money left at the end of the month, I'd use it to fly to Vegas for a weekend of gambling and partying. This is a prime example of *want* versus *need*, and it was a choice that cost me tens of thousands of dollars. The casinos gave me a false sense of importance by flying me on personal jets and "comping" my hotel rooms and bottle service (i.e. giving them to me for free). Why? Because I ended up spending more than what the rooms, flights, and bottle service cost!

It never failed—all that importance I felt on the flight to Vegas was replaced by regret and exhaustion on the way home. I soon began to realize that these wants were nothing more than a waste of my time, and more importantly, my resources. I remember winning $100, losing $100, winning $200, losing $200, winning $500, losing $500—and five hours later, I was right back where I started. I had just wasted half a day of my life that I'd never get back. In the end, none of it was fulfilling, even the few times I came back with more money than I had left with.

Not all wants are that unfulfilling—some of them can be both fun and enriching—but if your life is full of mornings spent wondering what you did the night before and how much money you may have spent, it's time to rethink the effect those activities are having on your budget.

I got the chance to ask Aaron Boone a few questions. Aaron played in the MLB for twelve years for the Cincinnati Reds (1997-2003), New York Yankees (2003), Cleveland Indians (2005-2006), Florida Marlins (2007), Washington Nationals (2008) and the Houston Astros (2009). He was an All-Star in 2003 and has transitioned well from his playing days to the world of media. He is currently an ESPN game analyst and regular contributor to the show, *Baseball Tonight*, which airs on ESPN.

DON: *Aaron knowing what you know now, what's the biggest mistake you see athletes make today coming into money?*

AARON: *Just the notion that this is the new norm for your life. Absolutely need to invest or put a healthy amount away as soon as you start making money.*

DON: *What's the best piece of advice you ever received when you were making money as an athlete?*

AARON: *When it comes to secondary items that aren't a significant part of your life—rent over buy.*

DON: *What's the best advice you would give a young athlete coming into money?*

AARON: *No matter how strong a position you think you may be in, plan for the worst-case scenario when it comes to money and your career.*

PART III: MANAGE CASH FLOW AND INCOME ALLOCATION

The final part of learning about your own money involves managing cash flow. Managing cash flow factors into your budgeting, but then it takes it a step further by giving you a way to measure your cash inflows and outflows in order to show you your *net cash flow*, also known as the "change in cash and cash equivalents."

Income and expenses are big drivers of net cash flow and generally include the following *cash inflows*:

- Salaries
- Interest from savings accounts
- Dividends from investments
- Capital gains from the sale of financial securities like stocks, bonds and or mutual funds
- Investment properties
- Business income

Essentially, cash inflow consists of anything that brings in money and can also include money received from the sale of assets like properties or businesses. *Cash outflows* represent all expenses. Cash outflows include the following types of costs:

FIXED COSTS (YOUR EXPENSES THAT REMAIN LARGELY THE SAME) SUCH AS:

- Mortgage or rent
- Property taxes
- Food
- Utilities
- Lease or car payments
- Debt payments
- School Tuition

- Insurance premiums
- Charity contributions and/or tithe

VARIABLE COSTS (YOUR EXPENSES THAT REGULARLY FLUCTUATE) SUCH AS:

- Personal care
- Dining at restaurants
- Entertainment
  - Sports and recreation
  - Going to the movies
  - Hobbies
  - Bars and clubs
- Children's schooling and activities

The most important step in managing cash flow is to find your *net cash flow* by subtracting your outflow from your inflow. (It is important to note that net cash flow is <u>not</u> the same as *net income*.) A positive cash flow shows you have extra income, and a negative shows you are at a deficit for that period. If you are at a negative, there will come a point when you will have to borrow money to keep up with your lifestyle— or declare bankruptcy.

Net cash flow is the fuel that helps people plan for the future, invest in the stock market or business ventures, and reduce debt. It is also what allows you to conduct the day-to-day business of your life. This is why some people value net cash flow more than just about any other financial measure.

I am a firm believer in the "Law of Attraction." Chances are, you've heard of the Law of Attraction, and if so, you may be wondering what it has to do with knowing your finances. Well, the short answer is it has EVERYTHING to do with your finances! Whatever you focus on with your mind, your time, your words, and your resources—it grows. If you focus on your Net Worth (Assets – Liabilities = Net Worth), it will grow. When you consciously track your cash inflows and outflows and commit to making your net cash flow grow, it will!

Dana Hammonds knows a lot about making SMART goals. She is the Senior Director, Player Affairs and Development at the NFL Players Association. Dana is all about service and gratitude and has been with the NFLPA for over 25 years. Her favorite part of her career is "being able to positively impact the players' lives. She does this by having oversight over the various divisions that provide services, whether its collegiate affairs, career counseling, or just regular player affairs and financial education, which is her core area.

I had the honor of interviewing Dana about players setting SMART goals when it comes to their finances. Here is what she had to say:

DON: *Dana, you are admired and looked up to by many of your players. What's the best guidance you received when you began making good money that you can give to athletes?*

DANA: *NFL players are no different than anyone else who experiences a sudden shift in their financial situation. Whether you are going from abject poverty as a college student to a job with a steady income, the psychological impact is the same—you have visions and dreams of what you want to do with your newfound wealth. The best advice I ever received is that you can have anything, but not everything. So make a plan and prioritize how you will spend your money by identifying purchases that need to be made now, and those that can be made soon and even later. Incorporate this into* *your budget and you have found a way to achieve your wants without breaking the bank.*

DON: *So many young athletes, like much of America, have never been educated in finances. What advice can you personally give to those who have little to no experience with managing money or setting SMART goals with their finances?*

DANA: *My advice to young athletes who have little experience managing money is as follows:*

1. *Educate yourself on personal finance. Begin by reading basic books or articles on personal finance. These books/articles are filled with information on how to save, plan, budget, invest and borrow in an easy, digestible manner.*

2. *Develop a savings/spending plan. A good budget will not only help athletes manage their day to day cash flow, but is a great technique to use to meet short and long term goals.*

3. *Build and maintain good credit. In football, scoring seven points is great, but shooting for a credit score of 700 is better. Maintaining good credit is essential for renting an apartment, purchasing a house or car and even getting great rates on insurance.*

DON: *In your 25+ years of the NFLPA, I'm sure you've
           seen it all with athletes, not just the NFL. What
           pitfalls would you advise athletes to avoid?*

DANA: *I have one piece of advice for all athletes: Don't
           invest in something you don't understand. This is
           true of investment vehicles, products or concepts.
           Take the time to learn about the investment before
           turning any of your hard earned money over.
           Basically, you want to have a good understanding
           of what you're putting your money into.*

Go to www.notanotherbrokeathlete.com to download a **Net Worth Tracker**. It will help you keep this important activity at the forefront of your mind (whether you do it yourself or have someone else track and report back to you on a regular basis). The point is to focus on increasing those numbers, cutting expenses when you can, and believing that the SMART goals you have set for yourself are worth attaining for your future and your family's future.

In college I never realized the opportunities available to a pro athlete. I've been given the chance to meet all kinds of people, to travel and expand my financial capabilities, to get ideas and learn about life, to create a world apart from basketball.

—MICHAEL JORDAN

4

Seek Counsel, Not Advice

When it comes to your money, whom do you trust? Do you seek counsel by hiring a professional like a Certified Public Accountant (CPA) to do your taxes, or do you take advice from your second cousin Ray-Ray because he's the smartest person in the family? For the purposes of this book, we will define *advice* as opinions given on a subject (such as your finances) with no background or expertise in the matter. We've all experienced such advisors in our lives. In fact, it's a good thing you didn't listen to people's "advice" when they warned you that you'd never play in the pros.

The most important thing to remember when it comes to knowing your finances is that you don't have to do it alone! Although this book is filled with information and ways to help you become more comfortable taking control of your financial future, there are professionals out there who can walk you through the process so you can go about your life with clarity and confidence in what lies on the road ahead.

What you don't need is more "advice." What you need is *counsel* that comes from your own personal *Financial Dream Team*. This Dream Team should include a great Certified Financial Planner™ (CFP®), a Certified Public Accountant (CPA), and a skilled attorney for your particular situation.

WHY HIRE A CERTIFIED PUBLIC ACCOUNTANT?

It is important to have a knowledgeable and helpful Certified Public Accountant (CPA) on your side. I hired a CPA in the past who was very good, but he always made me feel like I was bothering him. It was as though he didn't enjoy his work—or maybe he just didn't like me. Whatever the case, I finally found someone with whom I felt more comfortable and appreciated, and I did not have to feel guilty when I called him with questions or concerns. The primary reasons you need a great CPA are:

1. **Tax Planning.** You don't want to wait until April to see if you are going to get money back or owe more. It's a good idea to meet in June and then again in early December to get a tax estimate and ascertain whether you are going to pay money or receive a refund. During those meetings, you can get suggestions from your CPA and make adjustments before the year ends to better your tax situation.

2. **Tax Issues.** You will most likely face some tax issues in your career, which makes having a CPA on your side invaluable. The issues can range from an intimidating letter from the IRS to a full-blown audit. It's best to be proactive and have an expert

CPA on your team so that when you do encounter tax issues, you aren't scrambling to find someone.

3. **Retirement Planning.** A great CPA should be working in conjunction with your Certified Financial Planner™ (CFP) to make sure you are maximizing your tax deductions and saving for your retirement. This becomes especially important if you have other businesses other than your sports profession, where you can legally shelter a lot of money and save in tax-deferred growth.

If you don't already have a CPA or you are not sure about the one you have hired, here are some questions to ask when choosing a CPA:

1. How many years have you been in business, and how long have you worked for this firm (if appropriate)?
2. What is the average response time from you and/or your company?
3. What computerized accounting systems do you use, and are you familiar with other accounting systems?
4. How often are your clients audited?
5. Are you currently representing any other well-known athletes or celebrities (they won't be able to disclose names, but they can tell you whether they represent other athletes)?
6. What references and recommendations can you provide to help with the decision of who to hire for my financial team?

WHY HIRE A CERTIFIED FINANCIAL PLANNER™?

Over the last decade, we have experienced some rough financial periods in this country and worldwide. We had subprime mortgages, The Great Recession, the discrediting of the "too big to fail" theory, periods of extreme quantitative easing (also known as printing money),

George Bush, Barack Obama, trillion dollar annual deficits, stock market volatility, the social media revolution, smartphones, iPads, and Kim Kardashian.

It's been a wild and unpredictable ride, and because of that, financial advisors are no longer simply giving financial advice or doing nothing more than passively building your portfolio. The times call for an expert who can become the "quarterback" of your financial team. According to CFP.net:

> *CFP® (Certified Financial Planner™) certification is generally recognized as the highest standard in personal financial planning, qualifying financial planning professionals to provide their clients with comprehensive financial advice.*

A Certified Financial Planner™ is so much more than a person who knows how to help you plan for retirement. A CFP can assist you in:

- Determining your goals and expectations
- Analyzing your current financial situation by looking at your financial health, which includes examining your assets, liabilities, income, insurance, taxes, investments and estate plan
- Developing a comprehensive financial plan to meet your financial goals by looking at opportunities and building on existing strengths
- Implementing your financial plan and, just as important, monitoring it
- Keeping you on-point to meet changing goals, personal circumstances, fluctuations in the stock and bond markets, and the ever-changing tax laws

Hiring the right team or counsel isn't a foolproof plan. When it comes to your money, there are no guarantees that your financial advisor will always look out for your best interests every step of the way. If you want proof, just ask Terrell Owens. In 2013, T.O. sued his financial adviser, a South Florida bank, and others for mismanaging his finances. However, there are some strategic and important steps you can take to protect yourself and minimize the risk of being a victim of improper planning.

First, hire a financial advisor who is a CFP®. For a financial advisor to become a CFP®, he or she has to complete the four E's: *Education*, *Examination*, *Experience* and *Ethics*.

- **Education.** He or she must complete comprehensive courses in financial planning offered by a college or university program approved by the CFP board.
- **Examination.** The CFP® Certification Examination is designed for the financial advisor to assess his or her ability to integrate and apply a broad base of financial planning knowledge in the context of real life financial planning situations. By passing this exam, this person demonstrates to the public that he or she has attained a competency level necessary to practice independently as a financial planner.
- **Experience.** One thing you can't fake is experience. He or she needs to have at least three years of financial planning experience that has been verified.
- **Ethics.** He or she must abide by the CFP Board's code of ethics and additional requirements as required and are held to a higher standard of duty. This means a CFP® has a fiduciary responsibility to you, which means this person must act in your best interest.

It's also a wise idea to run an advisor or broker check. To do so, simply go to **finra.org** and click on "broker check" on the homepage. Every registered representative will have a record detailing his or her licenses, experience, and complaints (both paid out or rejected). This is like a credit report for *registered representatives,* also known as financial planners, financial advisors, wealth managers, or financial consultants.

After you've done your due diligence, it's time to trust your instincts. Ask yourself questions like: *Is this person here to educate me? Do I get the sense that this individual cares about my family and me? Is he or she just in it for the money? Do his/her values line up with mine?* There is nothing wrong with treating your first meeting with CPAs and CFPs like an interview. In fact, you should! There are many CFPs who specialize in helping niche markets such as professional athletes.

All of us, no matter what profession or industry we are in, need mentors and professionals in our lives who have "been there, done that" and who are experts in their fields. I know this is true for me, and I met one of the greatest influences in my life at a conference where I was a sponsor. He was a featured speaker at the conference, and at one point during his talk had the whole audience in tears, then laughter and joy as he was raising money for a charity that gives backpacks to the homeless (he raised over $50,000 that weekend).

Fast forward over two years later, James Malinchak has become a buddy and a mentor and who PS&A Wealth Management, Inc. goes to for business consulting. From living in a small Pennsylvania steel-mill town to being featured on ABC's hit TV show, *Secret Millionaire,* James Malinchak is a true American success story! James is recognized as one of the most requested, in-demand business and motivational keynote speakers and marketing consultants in the world. He also co-authored the bestselling book, *Chicken Soup for the College Soul* and was twice named "College Speaker of the Year." James has delivered over 2,000 presentations for corporations, associations, business groups, colleges, universities and youth organizations worldwide and can speak for groups ranging from 20 to 20,000. He created his business from scratch without being famous, having any advanced academic degrees and without any speaker designations or certifications from any speaker associations.

James is the behind-the-scenes, go-to marketing advisor for many top speakers, authors, celebrities, business professionals, entrepreneurs, sports coaches, athletes and thought leaders and is recognized as "The World's #1 Big Money Speaker® Trainer and Coach," teaching anyone who wants to get highly-paid as a motivational or business speaker how to correctly package, market and sell their time, knowledge, experience, expertise, message, personal story and how-to advice. I'm proud to feature some of James' advice in *Not Another Broke Athlete!*

DON: *You've been an athlete all your life. You've played in the Dapper Dan Roundball Classic, Division 1 College Basketball, and you even have a childhood friend that was Heavyweight Champion of the World. Today you also do professional speaking and business consulting. What's the biggest mistake you see athletes make today in regards to their finances?*

JAMES: *Two things: First they never plan for the future and have a "Plan B" in case their athletic career gets derailed, due to an injury or possibly just not being good enough to advance and play at the next higher level. Secondly, they rarely save their money and put it away, or at least a certain amount for the future. That's why you see so many broke athletes. Rather than saving their money, they often make* *"crazy" or outrageous purchases for things they don't need that put them in debt! My advice is to save your money and avoid or get out of debt as soon as possible! You can't create financial peace of mind with the burden of owing money.*

DON: *You even coach some of the coaches who coach athletes. So, what's the best advice you give to your coaching clients to protect and grow their legacy and to these young athletes of today?*

JAMES: *Stop blaming any lack of achievement on outside factors such as other people, the environment, the economy, a geographical location, etc. Take responsibility for what you are or aren't achieving in your life, and then take action to overcome the challenge and better your life and the lives of those you come in contact with!*

DON: *You've coached and mentored many people from all walks of life: from financial advisors, high performance coaches and athletes to even a Harvard trained physician and business owners. What is next for James Malinchak?*

JAMES: *My mission is to help people enrich their business and life. In order to help more people, including athletes, I have over 20+ online video trainings, speak for numerous organizations (including athletic-related) and have written 20 books. As a courtesy, anyone can get a free copy of my game-*

changing book, "Millionaire Success Secrets" by visiting: www.MillionaireFreeBook.com

You owe it to yourself and your family to find someone who both understands your situation and genuinely desires to make it better. With the right team on your side, knowing your finances and learning how to secure your future is easier than you think.

I'd love to have a lasting impact as far as growing the game. It would be cool to be remembered as a major champion. I'd like to be remembered as a great golfer but also a great person, as far as growing the game and charity work. The whole well-rounded athlete.

—RICKIE FOWLER

5

Is There Life After Sports?

Many professional athletes believe their careers will never end—and who can blame them? Athletes have got a good thing going. As a professional athlete, you are among the most admired people in the world. Who wouldn't want that to last as long as it could? Well, I have some news for you:

Your career may not be as long as you want it to be—and at some point, it *will* end.

Since you know you will face this inevitability at some point, it may be helpful to assess how you currently look at your career.

Dr. Pat Allen is a celebrity and communication expert. She has devoted 44 years to helping men and women like you express their wants and needs with integrity and honesty, and to recognize and avoid the damaging ploys of intimidation and seduction.

Dr. Pat has been interviewed on television's *Eye on LA*, FOX-TV and FOX News, *Geraldo, George & Alana, Joan Rivers, Mars & Venus, Maury Povich, Mike & Maty, Real Women, Terry Bradshaw, The Home Team, Yolanda, I Love New York, The Millionaire Matchmaker,* and four times on *Oprah*! She is also a bestselling author of many books.

When she and I sat down for an interview, we talked about a key distinction that I want to clarify for you now.

Being a "career man" versus a "man with a career."

They may sound similar, but they are actually quite different.

A *career man* likes to make money, exercise power, and exude prestige. The most important things are his power and status. He wants to be respected, and he often goes about pursuing that in unhealthy and damaging ways (especially damaging to his personal relationships).

According to Dr. Pat, in order to get the respect he desires from his significant other, he has to first cherish his significant other. She will in turn respect him.

A *man with a career* wants love and a family with his career on the side. An example of this type of person would be Adam LaRoche. Adam was a professional baseball player who retired because he was told his son could no longer hang out with the team.

He left $13 million on the table and self-sabotaged his career.

You can be both types, but not at the same time, or Dr. Pat Allen calls that narcissism, which is what you develop when you want to be "cherished and respected at the same time."

Are you a man with a career or a career man? Either one can work, as long as you find a way to balance your career and your family life in a healthy way that works for everyone involved.

One of the things that make a career in sports so much different than those in the business world is that sports careers end decades sooner than "regular" jobs. For men, the average life expectancy is 76 years, and a woman's life expectancy is around 78 years. And so, even after 20 to 25 years of playing a sport (an athletic career length that is rare), you will still have at least 45 years left to live. This means that it takes real focus and planning to ensure that you are able to fund that much life after sports.

I interviewed Jacob Cruz, my childhood best friend and a former Major League baseball player who now coaches in the Arizona Diamondbacks organization and who also invented the LineDrivePro® Trainer baseball hitting aid, a popular training tool that is featured in major sporting goods chains. During our interview, we talked about the major mistakes athletes make with their money as well as what it's like to face the sometimes harsh reality that your professional career will end one day. Here is an excerpt from our interview:

DON: *What did you learn from making money as an athlete?*

JACOB: *I believe we learn from our own life's mistakes. We can be advised and we can see other's pitfalls, but it's not until we experience the action that a lesson is learned. I am guilty just as much as anyone of over spending money. Even though I was self-aware of the future, you can get caught up in the moment and say, 'I got the money. I deserve this.'*

I don't believe anyone gave me better advice than my own self after a night in Las Vegas. You wake up and ask yourself, 'Did I really spend that much money?' The money is all relative to the money you have or are making, so my amount of dollars is definitely south of what a Michael Jordan would spend, but still the thought today makes me want to puke. It's an expensive life lesson. Time passes and you get over it, and things change once you have kids. It became about them and how much we are able to put aside to help them in the future. I believe there has to be a certain remorse in spending that leads the person to make changes. If there is no remorse there will be no life learned lesson and thus the spending will continue until it all dries up.

DON: *What's the biggest mistake you've seen athletes make with their finances?*

JACOB: *The biggest mistake I see from athletes today has been the same mistake I have seen for twenty years. Athletes believe that they will play forever, that their career will never end—and so the money will keep flowing in. No athlete wants to think about when it will all end, but it always does. Somewhere, some team will come up and tap you on the shoulder and they will say, 'Thank you for the service as a player and good luck, but if you choose to continue to play, it won't be with the current team. It happens to everyone. Everyone will get fired!*

It's the few players that choose to ride off on a convertible on the field as they celebrate their last year of playing. A farewell tour like Derek Jeter experienced is for less than 1% of all athletes. Those fortunate to have made their money before the injury are the lucky ones. What this all circles back to is that the player never considers this. They spend without remorse.

I once heard a financial investor say that a basketball player he represented was going through $300,000 a month. That's over $3 million a year on what? Entourage, cars, women, clothes, and the best investment of all, jewelry. When some [athlete] says that he is getting anything made custom and that they can have it to him in a few days for an overpriced amount, the end of a career is always near.

[For me,] my strong-willed mind could keep playing forever, but my body was in pain, saying no. I kept saying that Father Time is a son of gun, and I had to transition into coaching and becoming an entrepreneur. I always had a plan that my career wasn't the end of something, but a beginning to a new chapter in my family's and my life.

Once your career ends one day (and yes, they all have to end sometime), you will be faced with many choices—and like my childhood friend Jacob, you will likely find yourself trying to decide the best transition for you and your family. If you have saved your money and made wise decisions, those choices may sound a lot like these:

- Should I start my own business and become an entrepreneur?
- What business or businesses should I invest in?
- Maybe I could pursue a new career in another field of interest.
- Perhaps coaching is for me.
- I want to become a motivational speaker and mentor kids.

- I made wise choices and can retire and enjoy life, knowing my future is secure.

Sounds like a lot of nice options, doesn't it? Ideally, you will decide what your life after sports will look like long before you retire so that you have everything in place when the time comes. These decisions are made exponentially easier when you seek counsel from trusted, reputable advisors and make sensible decisions based on proven financial principles. Only then you will be able to face your future with optimism. *Life after sports can then become just the latest chapter in a string of successful choices.*

The alternative? Well, it isn't so nice. In previous chapters, you read the cautionary tales of athletes whose post-career financial failures served to steal the joy out of otherwise stellar athletic careers. Instead of being able to face their futures with a sense of adventure and a "what's next" mentality like Keith from our introduction, they must live out the rest of their lives steeped in regret, wondering where it all went wrong.

Instead of being remembered for their athletic skill and performance, many of those players are now saddled with a legacy that no one would want—they are remembered for their poor choices, not their time playing a game they loved.

What kind of legacy do you want to leave behind?

No one can answer that question but you. If you want to be remembered for the athlete you are rather than be branded by your financial mistakes, you must first realize and accept that there is life after sports. So, do yourself a favor and take the following steps below today. You'll find that these steps apply to anyone, whether you are a professional athlete, an accountant, an entrepreneur, a bus driver, a nurse, or a stay at home mom:

- **Find Your Why.** Find a purpose in life that is greater than what you do for a living. Perhaps it is giving back to charity or helping kids. Give your life a purpose that extends far beyond what you do for a living.

- **Start Saving and Keep Saving.** Save a large percentage of your income (as much as 50% if possible) and never touch it during your career. A savings mindset will enable you to weigh the pros and cons of those extra purchases and unnecessary luxuries in life. Moderation is often the key and will help you save enough money to do all the things you want to do later in life.

- **Live Below your Means.** Live below your means, not above them. Translation? Skip the G6 and the summer home in France for now. You can still have a luxurious and comfortable life without breaking the bank.

- **Stick to your Budget.** You need a budget, whether you are making $50 million or $50,000 a year. You need to know how much money is coming in and out every month. This is the only way to ensure that your spending never escalates out of control and you don't find yourself with a white Bengal tiger or a house made out of solid gold (and no money in the bank).

- **Have a Contingency Plan (or Two).** Remember your body won't hold out forever. Have a plan B (and C and D) for what you will do after professional sports. If you have a degree in something that interests you, then stay current on that industry so that you have a greater chance of finding work in that field after your retirement from sports. You must know what you will do after sports, whether your athletic career lasts one, five, or twenty years.

- **Keep it Simple.** Don't be the kind of athlete who regularly lavishes extravagant gifts on family and friends and buys drinks for the entire bar or restaurant. Buy a few nice and meaningful gifts for people, but don't let it become a habit—or you may find that everyone around you will expect it all the time.

- **Don't Overestimate Yourself.** Don't equate having money with being good at managing it! Getting large sums of money at once tends to have the opposite effect that it should. Rather than think about all the ways to *invest* it, too many people think, "How can I *spend* it?" Know your limits and find someone to help you manage your money from day one.

- **Don't Underestimate Yourself.** You may not know as much as you want to about finances and money, but you are smarter than you give yourself credit for. Don't let anyone tell you that you aren't clever enough to figure out how to live your life in a smart and financially sound way.

- **Be Wary of "Sure Bet" Pitches.** Second-guess every "sure thing" investment that gets pitched to you. Trust your instincts. When something feels too good to be true, it probably is. There's really no such thing as a *sure thing* these days. Most (if not all) successful enterprises require tremendous work and dedication.

- **Diversify.** Owning a bunch of assets is different than owning a diversified portfolio of investments. The best way to ensure your money outlasts you and even your children is to have a well-diversified portfolio created that is actively managed by someone with you and your family's best interests at heart.

- **Never Stop Learning.** The most successful men and women in the world will tell you to never stop bettering yourself. You may think you made it to the top because you are a professional athlete, but remember how hard you had to work to get there—and remember that success in other areas of life besides sports will require that kind of dedication as well.

- **Limit Debt.** If you can avoid taking on debt to purchase items, then do so. A large amount of debt is not your friend. Pay cash when you can, and if you can't afford something without taking out of line of credit, ask yourself if you'd rather have that thing or be able to send your kids to college one day.

- **Seek Expert Counsel.** And finally, find a reputable financial advisor. Check his or her references and make sure this person or people will look out for your long-term well-being. On the topic of expert counsel, Jacob Cruz said it best during our interview when I asked him "What's the best advice to give to young athletes?"

Where do you start with this question? Don't buy a sports car that takes half of your signing bonus? Don't let your leaching friends tag along. Don't think that you are the main character from the TV series Entourage. I see it all the time. Young kids with money and the cars they buy. Half the time it's the parents who say, "Let me take care of your money." That becomes a problem quickly. The parents, for one reason or another, feel entitled to the money.

I think the best advice would be to choose a person carefully who deals with money. Think about it. We never learn in school about money—how to budget, how to invest. So why do we all of a sudden believe we are educated in making decisions with money? It's foolish. We want someone who will fight us when we want to spend the money. If you have someone who goes with the flow and proves no limits or boundaries on your spending, then they don't have your best interest at heart.

As a pro athlete, it may seem like you've struck gold, but we all know that many athletes' careers have a short shelf life. Even if you are one of the lucky ones who enjoys a long and lucrative career, you will still be faced with a moment in time when you will have to retire, whether you are ready or not. So, plan ahead and know what obstacles stand in your way, and arm yourself with the right knowledge, tools, and people you need to keep and grow the money you worked so hard to earn. If you haven't already, contact a professional today who can walk you through the process. You owe it to yourself and your family to plan ahead.

Is there life after sports? Absolutely—and it's up to you to determine what that life will look like. Ultimately, it will be as satisfying as you make it!

I had the opportunity to interview former football great Warren Moon, a man who has truly embraced the idea of making life after sports the best it can be! Warren was not only inducted in the Canadian Football Hall of Fame, but he was also the first African-American quarterback to be inducted in the NFL Hall of Fame. Today, he is a broadcaster for the Seattle Seahawks on both radio and television. He founded the Crescent Moon Foundation, which provides support for educational pursuits that benefit children most in need who have displayed a commitment to their community, and other charitable causes. He is also co-founder with David Meltzer and President of Sports1Marketing, where they align athletes, celebrities and businesses together to create financial abundance providing a win-win situation for all parties.

DON: *You were fortunate to play football well into your forties, which is highly uncommon today and even back then. As you are I'm sure aware, the average that a football player plays in the NFL is less than four years. What advice can you give to a current athlete about transitioning into their post-playing career?*

WARREN: *Make sure you have a plan before retirement comes. They need to understand the money from football won't always be there, and even the higher paying jobs after football don't even come close to what you are making as a player. Spend time figuring out what you would like to do, network with people who are doing what you think you might like to do and educate yourself.*

DON: *What do you see as the biggest financial challenges that most athletes face today?*

WARREN: *Players not understanding how to save money and how to live on a budget. This includes not spending all your money on family and friends.*

DON: *What was the best financial advice you were given and would like to pass on to the athletes of today?*

WARREN: *Learn to save money and have a plan for what you are going to do once football is done.*

DON: *You have so much going on, from being highly involved in giving back through the Crescent Moon Foundation and other charities, President of Sports1Marketing which helps athletes, celebrities and businesses succeed together to a color commentator for the Seattle Seahawks. If we were sitting here three years from today—and you were* *to look back over those three years to today—what has to have happened during that period, both personally and professionally, for you to feel happy about your progress?*

WARREN: *Over the next three years I want to continue to establish Sports 1 as a leader in the Sports industry, grow our company exponentially from where we have grown that last three years, and continue to create a legacy for me and my kids.*

Let Warren's amazing post-football career be an inspiration to you.

Joe Theismann knows something about finding success in business after sports. And if you know anything about football history or if you watched the infamous game in 1985 and you hear the name Joe Theismann, your body probably cringes a little. Lawrence Taylor, also known as LT, not only changed the game of football, but also changed the life of the Washington Redskins legendary quarterback Joe Theismann, when he sacked Joe and snapped his leg in a career ending injury on November 18, 1985.

Everybody saw this as a tragedy, except one person, Joe Theismann, who saw it as a blessing. Joe was being carted off the field in a stretcher and 55,500 plus fans stood and cheered for him as he had never heard before. That was the moment that Joe realized he needed people to be successful, and it wasn't about just him. Not only is Joe an NFL Great and Super Bowl champion, he is also a sports commentator on television and radio, an entrepreneur since 1975, author of several books, and also a corporate and motivational speaker.

Joe has had to learn firsthand how to deal with adversity, changing and reinventing himself constantly. In his paid talks, he gives passionate presentations of strategies for handling challenging circumstances and dealing with unpredictable change.

The topic of financial literacy in sports, as well as the changes an athlete experiences throughout his or her life has gained a lot of attention in the media. Recently,

I had the great pleasure of speaking to Susan Sember, who is the Executive Producer and Director of a full-length documentary, "Beyond the Game" (http://www.beyondthegamefilm.com). With a background as a litigation and sports law attorney and an undergraduate education in television and film from the University of Michigan, Susan is an award-winning film director, producer and writer of numerous documentaries and feature films. She is currently set to release "Beyond the Game, produced by Silverlight Films. A passionate advocate for athletes, Susan uses her art of filmmaking to make a difference. Her newest release has intimate interviews with professional athletes who share their never-before-told stories in a positive and inspiring light.

DON: *How many athletes did you interview for "Beyond the Game?"*

SUSAN: *I interviewed, on-camera, over 70 athletes during the 2-plus years of the film production. The current and retired professional athletes came from all sports, including but not limited to the NFL, MLB, NBA, WNBA, PGA, LPGA, NHL, MLS, FIFA and Olympics. They range from very high-profile Hall of Fame members to the "journeymen" of these respective sports. In addition to these pro-athletes, I also interviewed coaches, athletic directors, team owners, and university presidents, along with a supporting "cast" of financial advisors, agents,* *attorneys and others.*

DON: *What did you learn in this process?*

SUSAN: *The question might better be about how I was
         inspired and transformed in the process and how
         I hope the audience will be, as well. I discovered
         athletes are an undervalued resource by the public,
         in many ways. In reality, they are a tremendous
         asset to their communities. They are valuable
         "ambassadors" for worthwhile causes, who go on
         to create businesses and nonprofit organizations
         that give back. They are leaders who have a myriad
         of transferable skills from which we all benefit.
         So much more than being sports stars, they are
         creative, innovative and have gifts and talents
         beyond athletic acumen. I loved every interview I
         had with these athletes and the stories they had to
         share-not necessarily about their greatest moments
         on the field or court-although those were very
         engaging and fun-but rather about life, business,
         public service and finance.*

         *Athletes are often unjustifiably vilified and
         misunderstood. I hope the film humanizes them;
         that it raises awareness and understanding of this
         unique group, and causes audiences to relate and
         respond to the similarities that often occur within
         their own lives. My greatest reward was producing
         a film that allowed the athletes to tell their stories
         in their own words, without limits, demonstrating*

the relevance to all audiences. I think viewers of the film will be very surprised at the revelations made and seeing a side of these athletes they didn't know or could even imagine.

Although the landscape of financial literacy is changing rapidly and dramatically, there is still a huge need for education and outreach. Student athletes, as all students, can benefit from financial and life skills programs as early as middle school. For those who haven't had the opportunities or exposure of such programs, it is imperative that they receive this knowledge at whatever stage in life. It's never too early or too late.

All professional athletes, but especially the "elder statesmen" of the sports, have so much to share in their mentorship, advice and wisdom. Over and over, I was reminded of the powerful legacies each will leave…and for which I am honored to have been able to document on film.

Parents were at the top of the list when I asked each athlete who they were most influenced by in their journey. With that comes the reminder of the extreme responsibility parents have in shaping that athlete. If a parent doesn't have the financial literacy or life skills to pass onto the athlete, they, too, need the education and exposure to these topics.

DON: *What counsel can you give athletes?*

SUSAN: *As an independent filmmaker, I, personally, am not the one to provide advice, per se. However, I discovered and was impacted by so much throughout the filming. I am grateful for the opportunity to share some of the messages relayed by the film's interviewees that keep me passionate about bringing positive change:*

- *Don't be hesitant, embarrassed or too prideful to ask money related questions.*

- *Be involved in all decisions related to your finances, career, health and lifestyle.*

- *Don't leave those critical decisions to others.*

- *Keep learning throughout your life, in all phases-student athlete to pro to retiree.*

- *You are an "expert" in your sport and it's ok not to be in other financial or business subjects.*

- *Always remember you have the right to know and should ask lots of questions of these other experts and keep asking... no matter who they are or how long you've known them.*

- *For all athletes but particularly for the "first generation of success athlete," don't allow the pressures to perform, please family and friends, or keep up with your teammates or others' perceptions of what you should be… color your financial, career and personal life decisions.*

- *Maintain a strategic focus to network and establish relationships while you're still "in the game". It will create contacts that will make the next chapter in your life more productive, financially successful and happier.*

- *Treat your sport and your brand as a business. You are the CEO of both. Utilize trusted experts but you and you alone must be the final decision maker on all.*

- *For student athletes, emphasize the student over the athlete. Concentrate on your education, life skills and the part of your life that will remain with you long after the sport.*

The same advice would be given to the student athletes' parents, as well as their schools and universities.

- *Invest in what you know.*

DON: *Many athletes have aspirations to go into film or television. What would you say to them?*

SUSAN: *There are countless parallels between athletes and* artists. In my opinion, athletes ARE artists on many levels. I have truly enjoyed my collaborations with the professional athletes in this film, as well as in other projects. I appreciate their visual and creative capacity, work ethic, persistence and success driven orientation. Yet, many former athletes have tried to direct and produce their own television series or films, only to be faced with failure and financial loss. In most cases, they attempt to do something for the first time at the "Super Bowl" level of the industry. They don't know how to find the teams with the right expertise, want immediate results, and expect windfall profits without an appropriate business plan. Like any financial venture, that's a doomed path. After 16 years in law and 18 years in filmmaking, I have seen many scenarios that only come with experience. I would recommend finding a mentor, be open to learning and recognize that it's a high-risk industry. If filmmaking is your passion as it was with sports, never give up. That same tenacity will carry you in your endeavors in the tough times and ultimately, produce a winning project. Filmmaking is one of the most rewarding second careers you can have…as personally spoken by a "recovering lawyer"!

The Essentials of
Starting a Business

—

By Shkira Singh

There I was, sitting at a big corporate desk in a high-rise in Downtown LA. I had always dreamed of moving up the corporate ladder and being a highly successful businesswoman. As I stared out the window at the people walking in the courtyard below, I wondered if they were satisfied with their careers. I had achieved all my goals and thought when I got here, I would be truly happy. However, that was not the case at all.

In fact, I felt totally empty.

I had just gotten a supposed "promotion" and was now working with high net worth clients, but I felt like an overwhelmingly negative energy was sucking the joy and happiness from my life. I would happily walk into the office smiling at everyone, but no one would acknowledge me. Everyone buried themselves in their cubicles and refused to look up because they were afraid someone might *actually* want to talk to them. I felt like I was in the Twilight Zone surrounded by mindless zombies.

WHAT'S YOUR WHY?

I had to start asking myself that very question as I looked around me—and it's a question everyone should ask, whether you are a professional athlete, an hourly wage earner, or a business owner. As you transition from sports into other ventures, you also have to ask tough questions like:

1. Why are you in the business you have chosen?
2. Are you passionate about waking up every morning and going into your office?
3. How are you making a true impact on your clients or employees?

Having passion alone will not make a business profitable, but that passion will be important when you are going through difficult times. *Running a business is a form of artwork that you have to master every day.* I witnessed this firsthand when I started my first business. I opened an insurance agency, thinking it was going to be great to do investments and cross sell insurance to clients, all while making a ton of money.

Ultimately, the driving force that incited me to start my own business was the desire to have something my children could one day help me run or sell and support themselves with the profits. While that was a noble purpose, the problem was that I was not really passionate about being a financial advisor and did not really care about selling insurance. I just knew I wanted to have freedom from corporate politics and have a flexible schedule.

I did not really care what business I opened as long as it was profitable.

Classic rookie mistake.

The happiest and most successful entrepreneurs are in business for a reason larger than themselves. I believe this is because they are driven by passion, desire, and something much deeper and more meaningful than money or recognition. I had not yet realized that when I first entered the financial services world.

I had been wandering around searching for my WHY since college. I had chosen to major in psychology because I felt it was an area in which I could make a huge impact on people's lives. However, I soon realized after doing numerous internships in the psychology field that it was not what I was meant to do. For me, it was draining work that depleted me of all energy and vitality.

I could not imagine doing that for the rest of my life, but I did not know what else I could do. I was working at a local bank during college and was moving up quickly, thanks in large part to my sales skills. I was soon offered a position as the assistant to a financial advisor and decided to take it since the income potential was extremely high.

I remember having conversations with my superior and co-workers about how I really did not feel I was making any real difference in the world. Everyone thought I was crazy; the money was so good…why did *that* matter? I caved in to peer pressure and chose to ignore my feelings as I continued down an unfulfilling career path for the next fifteen years.

As much as I tried to fight it, there came a point when it did not matter how much I made or how successful I was. I simply felt like there was a void in my life.

You can own every material item you could possibly want; you can pay all your bills with plenty of money left for more toys and vacations. Those are GREAT things! But without understanding your WHY, it will never feel as good as it could to experience financial prosperity.

You can be tired, sick, and have total chaos around you—but with a strong enough WHY, you will do *whatever it takes* to move your business forward.

As we grow in business and in life, we also grow and change as individuals. And that means our WHY's will be constantly changing as well! So, it's important to stay in touch with your WHY and go back to it from time to time in order to stay on track, and perhaps more importantly, to continue to feel fulfilled.

As you embark upon life after sports, perhaps you are considering starting your own business or entrepreneurial venture. If so, there are six action areas that will help you find your focus and keep you moving forward:

1. VISUALIZE YOUR WHY

First, your own personal WHY must become real and tangible to you. Here is a great first step toward making that happen. Write down your answers to the following three questions on a piece of paper:

- What is the reason WHY you decided to start/join this business?
- What does that mean to you?
- What does your WHY say about you as a person?

Once you write your answers down, keep them in your office where you can see them. You'll probably notice a lot of the first things that came to mind are material things—and that's okay (and normal). You have to start at the surface before you can go deeper. As you go deeper, ask yourself questions like:

- What truly touches my heart?
- What did I love doing most during my childhood?
- What "tribe" (aka ideal client) do I want to focus on and why?

You'll see that things start making sense and you will become clear on what your WHY is. Keep your answers with you, and when you find yourself feeling discouraged, go to the list and remind yourself why you are here.

VISION BOARDING

One of the best and most tangible ways to materialize your WHY is to create a vision board that you can look at to remind you of WHY you do what you do each and every day. Simply cut pictures out of magazines, newspapers, or travel guides (or print them out from a Google search) that convey your dreams and desires. Look at your board every day to help give you the push you need to keep moving forward. It's also important to do a vision board every year; it's vital to not get too comfortable in your goals. Set higher ones every year. *When you create a vision board, you take ownership of your dreams, wants, wishes, and desires.*

Knowing what's truly important in your life will help you stay focused on the road ahead rather than on the obstacles that could stop you and your business. By following your purpose, you will know your sense of direction and will ensure fulfillment in your life.

And when you have a purpose, you can have passion.

2. STUDY THE MARKET/FIELD

Having a purpose and passion is important, but it will not guarantee a successful business. You also need to study the business you want to enter and become an industry expert.

Before opening my insurance agency, I should have worked as an employee in another agency before investing my life savings into my own. I had no background in the business, and I did not perform the proper research or spend time studying the market and the insurance business.

If you can, try to work as an employee for at least a year in the business you would like to enter. I was not only learning how to run a business, but at the same time, I also had to learn how the business itself worked. Working in the industry before making a large investment is also smart because it allows you to see whether you even *like* the field.

There are so many things I learned the hard way in the first years. For instance, I opened my storefront in an area that was not insurance-savvy and was known for having cutthroat rate battles. If I had talked to other agents in the area, I would have been better prepared.

3. RESEARCH YOUR CONSUMER

The best way to get the data you need is to get it yourself; do your own research. Study the behavior of your ideal clients so you can be prepared for their most common wants and needs, as well as be able to anticipate their common behavioral traits and reactions. For example, I did not take into account that my client market was known for not paying their insurance premiums on time, thus creating a lot of administrative work every month in the form of policy reissues.

Look at the goals you've set for yourself and analyze the products and/or services you offer. Think about how your products or services fulfill a need or solve a problem for a potential customer. Also, think about how you differ from other companies in your industry—in other words, <u>what makes you stand out?</u>

Broadly think about who might be interested and who may benefit from having access to what you offer. *Figuring out your selling point is the first step in identifying your ideal target audience.*

Next, think about what information you need to know and why. What do you need to know about your potential customers in order to reach them?

As you consult your business plan and decide who you want your audience to be, remember that it is ultimately about the customer. Don't think about whom you would like to sell to; rather, think about who is looking for the products and services you offer.

After performing research, create a customer profile. This is more than a brief statement; it's an in-depth description of your typical customer and includes demographic and psychographic information:

- **Demographic information:** This type of information may include age, gender, location, ethnic background, marital status, income, and more.
- **Psychographic information:** This type of information goes beyond the "external" and identifies more about a customer's psychology, interests, hobbies, values, attitudes, behaviors, lifestyle, and more.

Both types of information are essential for developing your customer profile. Demographic information will help you identify the type of person who will potentially buy your products and services—but the work doesn't end after you've identified your target audience. It's essential to continually perform research to stay current on market and industry trends and on your competition.

It's also important to see how your current and potential customers evolve. Before you begin marketing to your potential customers, make sure you know how you are going to track sales, interactions, requests for information, and more. All of these touch points are important to record. This information will help you identify trends, patterns, and possible areas of improvement, which will continually help your marketing efforts as your business matures.

4. UNDERSTAND YOUR COMPETITION

The next point of research will be your competition. Learn what they say and where they say it. You don't want to copy them, but you do want to be aware of what they're up to. If you can, watch their sales presentation and observe their displays, packaging, follow-up methods, and their products and services.

You need to know the ins and outs of your future endeavor. Try to find models that are already proven to work, and get your ideas from there. Connect with businesspeople who are in similar fields, and polish up on your business classes.

5. NAIL DOWN YOUR BUDGET

Finally, just as you need a budget for your personal finances, you need a sound budget for your business from day one. Having a budget is the key way to help you turn your dreams for business success into reality. It will help you track cash on hand, business expenses, and how much revenue you need to keep your business growing.

By knowing and committing these numbers to paper, your chances of succeeding with your business are helped by anticipating future needs, spending, profits and cash flow. It also may let you spot problems before it's too late and no longer have enough money for emergencies.

A budget should be created before you invest in a business. This will help you figure out how much money you have, how much you need to spend, and how much you need to bring in to meet business goals. Budgets can also help you minimize risk to your business.

You can use this information to adjust your plans or expectations going forward. A 12-month budget can be updated with actual expenditures and revenues each month so that you know you're on target. If you're missing the targets set out in your budget, you can use the budget by figuring out how you can reduce expenses, or increase sales by more aggressive marketing, or lowering your profit expectations.

The vital elements of a business budget include: Revenues, your costs, and your profits or surplus cash flow. A budget should be tabulated monthly. Sales and other revenue will help these estimates be as accurate as possible, but always be conservative if you do not know the exact numbers (you may use your projected sales revenues or last year's actual sales figures for a more conservative estimate). To determine your actual profits, the simple formula is:

DOLLAR AMOUNT OF REVENUE—TOTAL COST = PROFIT

Costs can be divided into three categories:

1. *Fixed costs* are those expenses that remain the same, whether or not your sales rise or fall.
2. *Variable costs* correlate with sales volumes.
3. *Semi-variable costs* are fixed costs that can be variable when influenced by volume of business.

Once you have profit estimates, you can also start to see if you can afford to expand or invest in other areas of the business.

6. UTILIZE FORECASTING

Your sales forecast is the backbone of your business plan. People measure a business and its growth by sales, and your sales forecast sets the standard for expenses, profits and growth. The sales forecast is almost always going to be the first set of numbers you'll track for planning versus actual use. This is what you need to do even if you do no other numbers.

Forecasting is mainly educated guessing. So, don't expect to get it perfect; just make it reasonable. There's no business owner who isn't qualified to forecast sales if you have done your research. Business owners work hard every day to grow their business and make it a success. It's important not to neglect taking long-term strategy and planning into account by getting caught up in the day-to-day operations.

Start by forecasting unit sales per month. Not all businesses sell by units, but see how you can break things down in your business to get a sales number. For example, accountants and attorneys sell hours, taxis sell rides, and restaurants sell meals.

Whenever you have past sales data, your best forecasting aid is the most recent. You can get started by projecting your two most recent years of sales by month.

Forecasting income is important if you want your business model to run smoothly. In doing so, companies can quickly see if they have sufficient overhead, are pricing their products and services correctly, and see what their gross profit margin is.

MONITORING ACTIVITY LEVELS

Tracking and publishing your numbers tells employees what's important. For example, if you track customer satisfaction, number of refunds, and average customer hold times, your customer service manager knows precisely how he is being judged and what to improve.

Keep in mind: Don't just look at your numbers to determine what needs fixing. Use them to pinpoint what's working well in your business and do more of that.

Most entrepreneurs don't know these details. Yet, if you start to track and understand the numbers in your business, you can quickly increase your sales and profits. Research indicates organizations that set goals are much more likely to achieve them. However, to achieve a goal, you must be able to properly measure your progress. By understanding how your business is doing in both revenues and profits daily, you can tell if you're on track to achieving your goals and adjust your plans as needed if you're not.

There are a handful of smaller activities that effect larger results. For example, the following are often key underlying issues for sales:

- Number of outbound sales calls
- Number of live connections
- Number of proposals given
- Proposal close rate
- Average price per sale

When sales are low, most entrepreneurs don't know what to fix to see improvement. By tracking each of these numbers, you can instantly know what to fix. Most entrepreneurs have a bad sales month, then look back to determine what caused it. Had the entrepreneur tracked his numbers on the underlying issues, he could have fixed the problem early on. For example, he might have learned that the number of proposals issued in the first week of the month was low and made sure more proposals went out the door. By understanding and tracking your numbers, you can measure whether your business is performing well.

Key Performance Indicators (KPI's) are quantifiable measurements, agreed to beforehand, that reflect the critical success factors of an organization. They will differ depending on the organization.

KPI's should provide visibility into current activity that could impact future sales team productivity. Tracking these indicators in the present will allow you to identify gaps and coach your team members, which will help you influence the outcome of those monthly, quarterly, and annual productivity numbers that are so important.

These actions are **KEY** to the success of your organization. These numbers are related to **PERFORMANCE** and can be clearly measured, quantified, and easily influenced by the members of your team. Then they are used as an **INDICATOR**; in other words, the numbers are something that provides leading information about *future* results. It might be a good idea to track the number of calls and the amount of time each sales maker spends with high value contacts in those accounts, and then set some specific expectations there that can be measured.

Tracking KPI's is the best way to identify and qualify sales maker performance. Salespeople might be staying busy and giving 100 percent effort every day, which can be mistaken as real productivity. Tracking KPI's helps organizations make sure sales makers are spending the right amount of time on the right activities.

The best businesses are not those that focus on merely earning money, but those that are clear about their main purpose. It is important for business owners to plan and budget in advance in order for the business to remain stable and grow. It is also important to have data for your business to understand the market and consumer. Taking these six steps will help you avoid the errors that lead to most businesses failing.

Make sure your legacy stays intact by putting as much effort and energy into your next career as you did your first.

22 Things Every Player Needs to Know Before Starting a Business

---

By Dr. James A. Verbrugge

Dr. James (Jim) Verbrugge is an Emeritus Professor of Finance in the Terry College of Business at the University of Georgia. He was also the Chairman of the Department of Banking and Finance in the Terry College of Business. Dr. Jim has been on 11 different corporate board of directors and is considered to be a financial services and technology industry veteran as he is on the FI Navigator's Board of Directors. He also serves on the NFL Players Association Financial Programs and Advisor Administration.

Dr. Jim was gracious enough to share these 22 points that are based on a presentation he gave at the NFLPA Financial Advisors Conference in New Orleans in 2012.

By reading and internalizing these points, and then committing to opening your business with the utmost care and due diligence, you could be well on your way to your next exciting adventure.

PART I: UNDERSTANDING THE BUSINESS VENTURE

1. Have the appropriate personal characteristics to start a business—passion, focus, good at organizing and allocating resources, integrity, comfortable living with "ambiguity," and the ability to adapt to the inevitable "bumps in the road" that will occur.

2. What type of business do you want to start? Why this type of business? Is it compatible with your interests and existing skill set?

3. Can you answer several basic questions about the "market" for the product or service to be offered by the business? WHO is the customer? How many potential customers are out there? WHY should they buy the product or service—that is, what is the value proposition?

4. How will you get the product/service to the customer? A key to success to any new venture is to have an effective marketing/distribution system coupled with good management.

5. What is the plan to get the first <u>PAYING</u> customer? Then the 10th? Then the 100th?

6. Since every business venture is selling *something*, someone in the organization must be able to do this effectively. In most cases in a small venture, this means the CEO/owner.

7. Who or what is the competition for this venture? "There is no competition for what I will do" is NOT the right answer!!

8. Understand the "business model" of the venture. That is, how will it generate a sustainable, recurring, and growing stream of revenue? Can you explain it to someone in a few sentences (aka your "elevator speech")?

9. Business models of new ventures do not last indefinitely. There will always be external challenges to the business, some of which may be fatal to the sustainability of the business.

10. At some point in the process of starting a business, you must prepare a business plan, which is a short document that summarizes the people involved, the business opportunity, the context, and the "deal."

11. It is important to understand the *barriers to entry* to the business—that is, how difficult or easy is it to duplicate what you are planning to do?

12. Have a clear understanding of the *margins* in the business—gross margin, operating margin, and net margin. Each is important for different reasons.

    Gross margin is the difference between revenue and cost of goods sold, or COGS, divided by revenue, expressed as a percentage. Generally, it is calculated as the selling price of an item, less the cost of goods sold (production or acquisition costs, essentially).

    Operating margin is a margin ratio used to measure a company's pricing strategy and operating efficiency. "Operating income" here refers to the profit that a company retains after removing operating expenses (such as cost of goods sold and wages) and depreciation.

    Net margin is the percentage of revenue remaining after all operating expenses, interest, taxes and preferred stock dividends (but not common stock dividends) have been deducted from a company's total revenue.

13. Having adequate cash and generating cash flow from the business are of critical importance. Cash and positive cash flow provide credibility. Running out of cash is usually the death of a new business venture.

PART II: STRUCTURING THE BUSINESS

1. Get a good attorney early in the process who is experienced in structuring a new venture. This is just as, if not more, important than having a good accountant.

2. If there is more than one person involved in this venture as an owner or partner, be crystal clear about the ownership percentages at the outset. "We will figure this out later" is inevitably disastrous.

3. If there is any outside investor money in the business, be keenly aware of the expectations and risks created by the use of outside investor funds and outside investors.

4. Commercial banks are reluctant to lend money to a new business. If a bank is willing to do so, it will require personal guarantees and/or significant collateral that are not in the business itself.

5. Understand the difference between an *entrepreneurial venture* and a *small lifestyle business*—which are you trying to achieve?

PART III: LEAVING AND/OR SELLING THE BUSINESS

1. What if you want to sell what you started? How easy or difficult is it to get out? It depends to a large extent on, among other things, the nature of the business, the ownership structure, how the business was financed at the outset, etc.

2. Selling a *small lifestyle business* can be extremely difficult. There are usually few potential buyers. If there are potential buyers, they will do extensive due diligence, require defensible financial

statements (usually audited) and records, and expect to see a stable and hopefully growing customer base that is generating a sustainable revenue stream.

PART IV: CONSIDER A FRANCHISE AS AN ALTERNATIVE

1. If any or all of the above make you nervous or uncomfortable, perhaps you should consider a really good franchise. A franchise is much more about executing an already-proven game plan, whereas starting a new business is more comparable to preparing a game plan without much information about the opponent.

2. Who will you ask for advice? Find the right financial advisor and steer clear of those offering "free" advice…because that could really cost you. Put your trust only in those who have the background that warrants your confidence in them.

CONGRATULATIONS!

Step one is complete! Now that you read *Not Another Broke Athlete,* you have the tools and exercises to break the "chains" of a poverty or scarcity mindset, also known as limited beliefs. You now understand living a rich life is not living with a lot of money but living a fulfilled life with purpose. Last, but not least, you now understand the importance of growing and protecting your wealth so you don't bankrupt; emotionally, spiritually and financially.

I want to make it as easy as possible for you to take control of your finances. I want to help you set up your very own Personal Financial Website. This will provide you with the tools necessary to organize your financial life. All you need to do is follow these simple instructions.

Step 1. Go to https://psawm.com/personalfinancialwebsite

Step 2. Fill in the form provided with all the necessary information

Step 3. Click the button to submit your information

You will immediately be given access to your very own wealth management portal that will help you stay connected with your finances in one simple consolidated view.

Your future is determined by your actions today. Take control of your success, take control of your future and right now take control of your finances.

ACKNOWLEDGMENTS

I would like to thank the following people for assisting me on my journey:

First and foremost, God, without my higher power, nothing is possible; with my higher power I truly believe anything is possible.

I would like to thank my family, Shkira, Naiya, and E. Surin. I am extremely blessed to have you three in my life and I really don't know how you do it.

I want to thank Bella, Reyna, Raquel, the Pilar Family and Miriam Taylor for being the support my kids can lean on when we aren't available. I also want to thank Octavia Lindlar (Ms. Outside the Box), Erica Stephenson who also plays a big part in Naiya's life.

I want to thank my late Grandmother, who always saw my greatness and no wrong, my late Aunt Yoli, who treated me like hers, and my late Uncle Andre, who taught me how to drive by slapping me on the back of my head when I wasn't paying attention. I want to thank my Mom, Irma for the tough love, tough lessons and the entrepreneurship, my stepdad, Paul, my Dad, and Donald for leading me to God at a very young age.

I want to thank my late Uncle Johnny, Aunt Brenda, Brandy, Brandon, Diasha, Caderion, Antonio and my Uncle Ronald. I also want to thank my brother and sisters, Eric, Crystal, and Alex. I want to thank my step family, Vanessa Bell, Walter Bell, Eric Bell and Christian Vance for always treating me like we were blood.

I also want to thank my cousins Linda, Tony, Andre, Levi, Cassie, Art, Jr., Adam, Ashley, Amanda, Patricia, Rebecca and Alyssa.

I also want to thank my Aunt Aida, Uncle Oscar, Uncle Art and Aunt Alma, where I always had a place to go even when I didn't have a place to go.

I want to thank Jimi, Rani, and Rishi Patel. I want to thank Sangeeta Patel Hira, Jai Hira, their twins and Naiya and E. Surin's cousins, Leela and Dhyann Hira.

I would also like to thank the Abbe Family, Singh Family, Cuevas Family, Dass Family, the Sappal Family and the Mann Family.

I want to thank all the amazing humans that I've had the privilege to share great moments with and some amazing memories, especially Meera Joshi Patel, that took my title "WGD," Amy Ablakat, Sagar Patel, Sylvia "Lorena" Cuevas, Omar "Victor" Barillas, Darsha Phillips, Shareena, Shetal Patel, Sheena, Shyamal, Nilay, Cesar Cruz, Ray C, BC, aka John Picard, Marcos aka Party Boy, Raychel Gomez, Arod Entertainment, Jimmy Duran, Naomi Honohan, Gio Munoz, Belen Romero, Gaby Vidrio, Maggie "Magic" Yepez, Cao Tri, BoF freaking Santos, Paul "Pablo Pared" Fenlon, Nina, Jason "aka Classic Man," Becky Jacquez, Laura Sapien, Sara Sapien, Joanna Jacquez, Reno, Boy Adrian and Girl Adrian, Ernie Goldstein, Sam Sy, Sam Mandel, Lee "Cracker," Jessikah C, Amber Anderson, Ken Griffey Jr., especially for that head butt that knocked me into the twilight zone, Mark Garcia, Fernando "always mad" Lopez, Joe, Jose "aka big feet Chepe," Paul Chopra, Cris Arredondo, Cristianna M., Cheyenne S, and whoever else that I have shared great times with.

I want to thank James Malinchak, the James Malinchak inner circle family, Jennifer Lill, Cristina and Eric Gomez without you this book wouldn't be possible.

I would also like to thank everyone that has contributed to the book, my brother from another mother, Jacob Cruz, Oscar De La Hoya, Aaron Boone, Dana Hammonds, Dr. James Verbrugge, David Meltzer, Warren Moon, Dr. Pat Allen, Dr. Mamiko Odegard, Dr. Tim Benson and Joe Theismann. I also want to thank the Morgan James Publishing Team and Tiffany.

I also want to thank, whom were God sent, Chris and Jim Howard, whom have gotten thousands of authors across the finish line and introduced me to the Morgan James Publishing family. I also want to thank my editor Nancy James.

I want to thank my main man Mr. Carlos Martinez, without this guy, not sure I would be sane and in one piece. Thank you to my other brother Rob Sett, in tough times he has been there. I also want to thank some of my closest friends, late Ricardo Trujillo, Sal Martinez, Bee Bee Cruz (aka Mrs. Blunt), Victor Medina, Ruben Gallardo, Frank Lopez, Rob Reyes and everyone who has contributed to me evolving as a human being.

I want to thank all the former and current John Hancock Financial family. James Lee, Fred Johnson, Walter Cho, Michael Parks, Edward, Julie Rhee, Sam Sy and all the others that had an impact when my career began.

I would also like to thank all the previous Wamulians, Chris Joyner, Phil Hurst, the Redwood City Team led by M. Teresa Ocegueda, who really opened the doors for me to be a successful financial consultant, the Culver City team led by Diana Nielsen and Lynn Brumfield, and the Alhambra team led by Ovi and Ray. I also want to thank Brad Marshall and James Wong who were mentors to me at that time. I want to thank all of the back office support and compliance including, Barbara and

Mike Tonkel, Calvin Kwan, Dawn Rybak and Lauren Stewart. I want to thank all my previous assistants at Wamu, Smansa Chu, Ellen Lou, William Tien, Scott Lam and everyone else I missed.

I want to thank the current and all the previous PS&A Wealth Management, Inc. team & PRV Wealth Management. Summy Shen, Patricia Shen, Alice Ting, Jennifer Lee, James Kaing, Robert Claros, Nadezh, Dorothy, Ting Ting, Cindy, Yadi, Rizky, Raul, Gabby, Nicole, Paul & Nancy Vega, Joe, Ricky, Alex and everyone else who played a part in the formation and the ongoing cultivation of PS&A, including all the interns.

I would like to also thank all my clients with PS&A Wealth Management, Inc., without you all, I would have never been able to live the life of my dreams. Thank you, thank you, and thank you for your continued trust and love.

I want to thank also everyone previously and currently working at LPL, without them I would have never become an independent advisor.

I want to thank the Kestra Financial Family, formerly NFP Advisor Services. Thank you Bill Tadio, James Poer, Jenny Menard, Heather Smith, Patrease Rogers, Mackenzie Grant, Stuart Silverman and the Fusion Team, Phillip P. and the entire Esemble Practice, Will Gallegos, Tom Wright, Shawn Gordon, Shawn Thompson, Jenny Menard, Scott Buckey, Leah Alter, Tricia Stringer and the commissions team and all the good "folks" at Kestra. The transition from LPL to Kestra wasn't pretty, but it was well worth it as Kestra truly "Empowers Their Advisors!"

I want to thank my Landmark Family, especially the Communication courses and Team LA led by Jen Herda. Thank you also Lilly Star leading the Wisdom courses.

I want to thank my Strategic Coach Family, led by Adrienne Duffy. Thank you Marilyn Prehbul, Jana Mackic and Barb Da Costa, for your commitment and opening the door to the "Launch" by Jeff Walker.

This ultimately led me to Morgan James Publishing and PS&A Internet Marketing.

I want to thank everyone in the NFLPA, as I already thanked Dana, but I also want to thank Jasmine Frazier, for her hard work and dedication.

I want to thank fellow Entrepreneurs and Superstar Internet Marketers Jeff Walker, Product Launch Formula, Russell Brunson, Dotcomsecrets & Clickfunnels, and Jesse Doubek, Facebook Guru and his team at FanPage Academy, Mitch, Jill and Ryan.

I want to thank Greg and Allyn Reid, the late Hilliard, Katrina T. and the entire Secret Knock family. These events truly did open a lot of doors.

Thank you, Jim Skrumbis, Stephanie Rubin, Jody Walker, Steve, Lynn, Mrs. Theo, Jody Walker, Kendall, Adam, all the teachers and everyone including all the parents in the Sierra Canyon School Family. I'm so proud of the impact that Sierra Canyon has made on Naiya (teaching her how to think in an environment that it is cool to be smart and most importantly, the values) and soon E. Surin will be going there. Sheesh the place makes me want to go to school there. "GO TRAILBLAZERS!"

Lastly, I want to thank the people that make me look good, or try to, LOL. Thank you to my trainers and previous trainers: Jeanette Ortega and the ERF Team, Raul Murillo of Coreathletics, Tony Tirado, and Rob Cook. Thank you to Dr. Christine Ibrahim, Kris Baghoomian, Andrea Henderson, Leandro DeLeon of L7 Hair Studio, Ronald Murphy of Mr. Scissors Barbershop.

ABOUT DON

Don Padilla is a CERTIFIED
FINANCIAL PLANNER™, public
speaker, author and CEO of PS&A Wealth
Management, Inc. He is also a National
Football League Players Association
(NFLPA) Registered Player Financial

Advisor and the author of the book, Not Another Broke Athlete, written
to help athletes grow and protect their legacy. He has taught and lectured
retirement courses at various universities and colleges.

Don has been in the financial services industry for over 18 years and
has advised over $300,000,000 as of February 1, 2017. He is a Registered
Representative with Kestra Investment Services, LLC, where he holds
his Series 7 (General Securities Representative), 24 (General Securities
Principal), 63 (Uniform Investment Advisor Law) securities as well as
his Life/Disability. Long-Term Care and Variable Annuity licenses. He
is registered in the following states: California, Nevada, Texas, Arkansas,
Idaho, New Mexico, North Carolina, Oregon and Virginia. He makes
it a point to treat everyone like family and guide to the "Wealth with
Integrity."

ABOUT SHKIRA

Shkira Singh is a Financial Advisor at PS&A Wealth Management, Inc. Shkira has been a trusted advisor to her clients, both individuals and businesses, for over 14 years. During this time, she has advised over $250,000,000 and is a Registered Advisor with Kestra Investment Services, LLC where she holds her Series 7 (General Securities Representative), Series 63 (Uniform Securities Agent State Law Examination), and Series 66 (Uniform State Law Examination), as well as California State Life and Health Insurance licenses. She focuses on advising high net worth individuals with retirement income planning, wealth preservation, as well as estate and family asset transfer strategies.

Shkira specializes in helping to simplify complex financial issues and present them in a clear and understandable manner. Her background in Psychology allows her to understand that everyone's economics and life situation is unique and believes it takes more than a "one size fits all" financial planning approach help her clients work toward reaching their goals.

She helps her clients work toward a balanced approach to their financial planning needs, and is well versed in all areas of investing including bonds, stocks, managed money, life insurance, annuities, mutual funds, 401k and retirement planning.

During Shkira's career, she has held positions at Washington Mutual, Farmers Insurance, and UnionBanc. Her academic credentials include a Bachelor of Arts in Psychology from the University of California Santa Cruz.

Shkira has a true passion for travel, hoping to explore as many countries and cultures as she can in her lifetime. Don and Shkira live in Porter Ranch, California with their two children. They enjoy spending time with their family.

DISCLAIMER

Kestra Financial, Inc. is the parent company of Kestra Investment Services, LLC (Kestra IS), member FINRA/SIPC and of Kestra Advisory Services, LLC (Kestra AS). Except for the referenced Kestra companies, Kestra IS is not affiliated with other entities referenced on this document. Kestra IS and Kestra AS do not provide tax or legal advice.

The opinions expressed in this book are those of the author and may not necessarily reflect those held by Kestra IS or Kestra AS. This is for general information only and is not intended to provide specific investment advice or recommendations for any individual. It is suggested that you consult your financial professional, attorney, or tax advisor with regard to your individual situation. If there are any comments concerning past performance they are not intended to be forward looking and should not be viewed as an indication of future results.

Morgan James
Speakers Group

➚ www.TheMorganJamesSpeakersGroup.com

We connect Morgan James published
authors with live and online events
and audiences who will benefit
from their expertise.

CPSIA information can be obtained
at www.ICGtesting.com
Printed in the USA
BVOW08s1518140218
508136BV00001B/1/P